The Nightlife Entrepreneur

Becoming more than a club promoter

JULIO MARIO ZAMBRANO

ISBN: 0997947217
ISBN 13: 9780997947212

To my wonderful wife, Rochy, who gives me the strength day in and day out to go on with my crazy ideas and ventures, even those that extend into never-ending nights. Also for always being my number-one fan.

To my unconditionally loving parents, Alvaro and Gladys, who encouraged and taught me from a very young age to become not only a successful businessman but also a better human being every day.

To my children, Pierre Angelo, Bruno, and Arianna, for teaching me what matters most in life and pushing me to get this project done before they were even born.

To my business partners, especially Gustavo "Quilla," for a long-lasting and healthy business marriage, where everything was not always perfect.

To my angels, both Mamis, Toto, Mimi, Toñi, and all who left this mortal world too early but have kept in touch with me ever since. You are the ones who guide me through when my path gets lost.

To my sister, Maricaro, who got me into this business without ever even knowing so.

To all the subpromoters, main promoters, club owners, club managers, bartenders, servers, hostesses, barbacks, bussers, security, and simply everyone who has been a part of this unforgettable journey.

To the hundreds of musicians and disk jockeys who kept our clients on the dance floor, mostly DJ Willy, who has been with us from day one.

Last but not least, to the millions of party animals who have contributed in making my life a fun and successful journey that is still going after two decades.

TABLE OF CONTENTS

Introduction   vii

1   Is This a Hobby or a Career?   1
      How serious are you about doing this? is it for you?

2   How to Be That Person   11
      How to get started in this beautiful business

3   Money Never Sleeps   23
      The importance of good money management

4   Size Matters   35
      Discussing your most valuable asset.

5   It's All about the Show   47
      Why people always come back to you

6   Use Your Weapons   57
      How to bring new clientele to your new business

7   It's Showtime!   67
      What to do on the day of the main event

8   Everyone's Best Friend   77
      The effect of your personality and your relationships.

9   Local Celebrities   89
      Handling your VIPs and controlling your ego.

10   Where Am I Now?   99
      Your lifespan as a nightlife entrepreneur.

INTRODUCTION

If I had a dollar for every time, I was approached at a nightclub by someone who wished he or she had my job, I would probably be retired by now. Actually, come to think of it, I might just have made a few more dollars from him or her already. I mean, the average cover charge nowadays at a nightclub is around twenty bucks, and the people who say they want my job so badly must have already paid that charge a few times. Then there are the friends or guests who did not pay the cover but who must have spent some money at the bar or the VIP tables. In that case, I made an average 20 percent of what each of my friends spent inside the club, which most likely was a bit more than twenty dollars. All the while I did not have to spend a dollar on my VIP table, the one with all the beautiful people having the time of their lives. OK, I get why people want my job. Wouldn't you?

I have been in the business of nightclub and bar promotion since before I was even allowed in one. I started when I was fresh out of high school, so that's twenty years and counting. I decided to write this book, *The Nightlife Entrepreneur*, for a few reasons. The first was just a longtime need to write something. For the past twenty years, I've been writing promotional material to get my friends and clients excited about coming to the nightclubs that I promoted, and almost every time I sent out those text messages, I got messages back from a lot of the recipients telling me that I should write a book. Some said I should write poetry. Some said I should tell stories about what happens in the nightclubs...you get the drift. Luckily for you, I'm no Shakespeare, so you won't find poetry here.

A couple of months ago, I received the great news that I was going to be a father. This made me extremely happy, since it is something I have dreamed of for a while now. My wife, Rochy, and I are expecting our first child this coming November, and I just can't wait to meet him. Despite everyone believing it would be a girl so that I could pay for all the bad choices I have made in the past, it's a boy. And no, I have not done as many bad things as some say I have. But why don't you be the judge of that as I tell you more about my journey?

The second reason I decided to write this book is my son Pierre Angelo. I want to leave some kind of legacy for him and his generation in case they want to follow in my footsteps. He is not only why I decided to write the book, but he is also the reason I decided to stop procrastinating and do it now. At the time I'm writing this he is due four months from now, and this being my first book, I have a hard road ahead if I plan to finish before he gets here.

Last but not least, this book is written to help people like you get rid of their fears and learn from my mistakes in order to start their own business and happy lives.

In this book I will share most of what I have learned in the past twenty years, but more than anything else, I will help you get started in what has been for me the most amazing career, one that everyone else wishes they had. Let me help you become more than a club promoter—become my fellow nightlife entrepreneur.

1

IS THIS A HOBBY OR A CAREER?

Most people who talk about promoters, especially nightclub promoters, think of them as pursuing a hobby or, for those who take it more seriously, a part-time job at best. Even though this is a possibility and it works for a lot of people, I decided to go a different route and make a career out of it. In the end you choose what you want this job to be. In order to make that decision, you need to make sure you know what you are getting into.

The first thing you need to know is that even though most people will say they want to trade places with you, this is not the reality. There are a lot of things that you will give up, as you become a promoter, at least if you want to be a successful one. The people who tell you they want your job are only interested in the part they are used to seeing in the clubs. They are saying this because they believe that you just get paid to party. OK, this might be a little true in the beginning, since most promoters start at an early age, and at that time of our lives, we are only thinking of the weekend, the opposite sex, and being popular or the center of attention.

In my case I started promoting in high school, back in 1993 when a couple of friends and I attended another high school's open house party. Open house parties were very popular back in the '90s in Miami. We went to this party and saw that there was not much to what these guys were doing. The guys who were throwing the party were college students—freshmen, to be exact—and they had come to our school to promote to the girls in the senior class. Renzo, one of my best friends, had an older brother who happened to be good friends with some of the college guys who were inviting our high-school girlfriends to the parties (well, not girlfriends, but friends who happened to be girls). I was not the most popular guy with the ladies back then, and neither was my group of friends—go figure. So we decided that it would be a good idea to copy what these college guys were doing and invite not only the senior class but the sophomores and freshmen as well.

Within a couple of weeks, we were throwing the first party at our friend Tuco's house. There were not that many people, but right away we realized that there was so much potential to do this on a bigger scale. Two weeks went by, and we were dying to throw another party, but we did not have a place to do so this time. My friend's parents found out that we had used their house when they were away on vacation in Ecuador, and this did not help a bit with our plans.

The following week the college guys had another gathering of college and high-school students, but this time there were a lot more people at their open house. They were charging a dollar a beer, and they did not check for ID at all. This not something I encourage today. We could not believe what we were seeing. But right before I was able to get to my second beer of the night, the party came to an end as everyone started running outside, throwing their Solo cups, and screaming, "Cops, cops, let's go!" Renzo's brother, who had brought us to the party since it was at his friend's house, was nowhere to be found. We looked around the backyard, since these events were usually held there instead of inside, but we didn't find him there either. We decided to go inside and wait for him to come back for us. As I waited, I realized, the owner of the house was extremely pissed off that the cops had shown up. Not only had they come to ruin the party, they also told him that the person who had called them was a next-door neighbor who said there were underage kids drinking at this party. The cops said that if they got any other complaints, they could come back and arrest the owner of the house if the allegations were true. Besides being mad at this neighbor over the accusations, the owner was mad because he did not make his investment back on this party, even though he'd had more people than the last time.

This was a very important moment in my life and my career, as it was the moment when an idea first came to me. It stuck with me for the next week, and then I came up with an even better idea that could work if done right. I met with some of my friends and told them about my crazy idea, and surprisingly, they were all very interested in putting it to work. We decided that we would throw another party in the next week or two. Our first mission was to find a house. We'd already had problems at Tuco's parents' house, so that was out of the question. My house was not even in consideration because my parents were not so thrilled with the idea. So we started talking to everyone at school who had a house with a big backyard, which was not hard to find in the Pinecrest area. The person also needed to be interested in making some extra cash and building up his or her popularity in school. This was probably the biggest seller of the whole deal; remember, this was high school, where it is all about the popular kids. The hardest part was finding someone who would be home alone. The parents had to be out of town for the weekend in order for this to work.

Well, it was not as hard as I thought, since there were over four hundred students in the senior class alone and over twelve hundred in the school. We did not care if it was a senior's house or not; we just needed the house for our great idea.

The following week we had not only secured a house for that weekend, but we also had a list of houses available for different weekends of the year. This made me think of the second part of the plan right away: Why do this in one spot alone? We could move around, and that way we would not have to worry about the cops coming back to the same house for complaints. Well, at least this is what we told the owners of the house. We said, "This is a one-time deal. We don't want to do it more than once so you don't get in trouble." These made them feel even more comfortable with us, and it helped build trust.

But our plan was very different from what we were telling these kids at the time. We could not do these events twice because it was not good business for us. We knew that we had to move around. So this was the plan: we'd get a house, make sure the parents were out of town, and make a deal with the owner of the house where he or she got to keep 25 percent of the sales and the reputation for throwing great parties.

Part two of the plan was the cover charge. Instead of having no cover at the door and one-dollar beer cups on the patio, we decided to charge five dollars at the door for a red Solo cup and all-you-can-drink beer. The main reason for this was that it would attract more people, since we were promoting an all-you-can-drink event. Most kids thought they could drink all they wanted, even though we already knew they could not handle more than a couple of beers anyway. Everyone loved the idea, but no one as much as my partners and me, who were the only ones who knew the most important detail of the business: we knew that the kids were not going to have more than two beers, because we knew the cops were going to show up. And the main reason we knew this was because we would be calling the cops ourselves. We knew that right about midnight, it was usual for the cops to get calls from neighbors complaining about noise or cars parked on other people's lawns. So we decided that we would make anonymous calls using neighbors' addresses and complaining about the noise. By the time the cops arrived, we would already be gone, and all the money would have been charged. This became such a good business that we later added the option of hard liquor for ten dollars in a different-color cup, as well as live music provided by local high-school bands that did not charge us to play. The parties became so famous that we now had kids from every high school within a thirty-mile radius attending, and even the college kids were coming to our parties. This is how my journey began in the event- and nightlife-promotion business.

By the time I was out of high school, I had already become way more popular than I had ever been. I'm not talking about being popular with the ladies alone; I mean I was popular among everyone in the high school, and I even had friends in over six other high schools. Even the teachers knew who I was. For some reason these parties helped me gain some kind of self-confidence that I did not know I had. I never thought that throw-ing a few parties in high school with young kids would ever take me where it did, but it would be the base of my business in years to come and helped me become self-employed at an early age.

Unfortunately high school was not forever. As I left for college, it became a lot harder, since I was not the big shot I had become in high school anymore. I had to start making a name for myself again if event promotion was going to be something I did more often. The hard part was getting the college students excited about going to open house parties and listening to local bands that sounded more like elementary-school bands. But very quickly I realized that this was what I wanted to do. I missed throwing parties, I missed being popular, and I missed making money so easily. Basically I missed getting paid to party.

It was in my second semester of college when I went to my college counselor and told him what I was experiencing. At the time I was going to school for accounting. Out of all the possible careers out there, I went with accounting. For some reason I did not pick my career at the time based on what I loved doing but rather on what I was good at in school. I was really good with numbers—so good that a few times I helped my accounting teacher give the class to sophomores and freshmen. It was due to her recommendation and my parents' approval that I decided to start studying accounting. It would have been a good career choice if I had loved handling other people's millions of dollars and if I loved cubicles and nine-to-five jobs. These were all things I considered normal, yet they never really became part of my life. You can imagine that I am not a morning person at all, as any promoter who takes his or her job seriously will tell you. Besides, why wake up early if everyone else who works with you is still asleep anyway?

That day the counselor asked me what I loved doing the most, what I saw myself happily doing for the rest of my life. And I bluntly said, "Well, I love to party. Is there a career that pays me to party? How about becoming a promoter? I could promote nightclubs, concerts, events, and all kinds of parties. What do I have to study in order to do that?" And all he did was laugh and say, "Come on; seriously, that is not a career. There must be something else you like." I sat there in front of him for two more minutes in complete silence. Then I left, saying on my way out, "It should be a career."

I can't say I was not disappointed at the time. I went home with a sense of worthlessness and extreme boredom with the way my life was looking at the time. But I could not sit down and let this stop me from making my dream a reality. How could it be that I had made this a business in high school, and now this person who worked for the university and was there to help me choose and plan my future was telling me that my dreams were just that—dreams? This was kind of like telling a kid that his or her lemonade stand is a dumb idea. Well, I'm sure the kid with the lemonade is not going to let the lemons rot if life keeps throwing lemons at him or her. I was not only in love with what I did in high school, but I also realized that I was good at it too. And all it took was looking at what someone else was doing, fixing what was not working for him or her, and making it a little better. There had to be a way for me to do this on a bigger scale, I thought. Fortunately I realized that where there is a will, there is a way. I will never forget that day. I made a decision to continue my studies, since this was still going to help me promote whatever it was that I decided to promote later in life. And without a doubt, accounting was a career choice that did help me in starting my business. No matter what business you decide to go into, I recommend that you take a few accounting lessons. Numbers and money are what we do most of it for. In order to be really happy, though, you need to be driven by something other than money. At this time in my life, I was still not sure what that was. Back then I was doing it more for the money and the fame or popularity. I will say that is not the case today, but I will get into that much later in the book. Money comes on its own when you love what you do.

The main purpose of this chapter is to differentiate between promoting as a hobby and promoting as a career. Like I said at the beginning, either way is OK. It is completely up to you to decide what you want this to be, and this book will help you with either path. But my story is proof without a doubt that this can be as much a career as any other that you spend years studying in college and university. The problem is that this career is not taught at any college or university program anywhere around the globe. That is why I have never felt guilty about quitting college before graduating, since I did not choose to quit. I simply chose a career that might not have been given attention by schools but that does exist, and the only place I could learn it was on the streets, hands on, doing what I loved and learning from others who did the same. I also learned from my own mistakes and from those I picked as mentors on the way. Believe me, there will be a lot of possible mentors who will drag you down more than help you in this business. But if you don't give up, you will run into the right ones, and they will help guide you in the right direction, sometimes without even knowing all that they are doing for you. I have a lot of people to thank for getting me where I am today, which is another reason why I've written this book. But I'll do that later, when we meet them in this story. For now, let me thank the counselor who didn't believe and is now one of my best clients.

I want to make sure you understand that I am not recommending that you quit school or that you pick this as a career. This is my case, and it worked for me. If this is something that excites you, if this is something you would love to do every day and call it work, then follow all these steps, and you won't regret a thing. As a matter of fact, now that you have picked up this book and are considering this as a career, you have a lot more options than when I was getting started. Who knows, maybe by the time you read this book, nightclub promotion and production will finally be offered as a career option in colleges and universities, as it should be. I promise that I will do my best to make that happen, but until it does, I offer you as much help as I can to become the best nightlife entrepreneur out there.

When I started this chapter, I talked about promoting as a career and how a lot of people say they wish they had this job, yet they don't even know what it is that we do. Even worse, they don't have a clue about all the things we have to give up when we sign up for this job. I want to make sure that you understand all the negative sides of this business before I get into all the positives. Let's start with the most common thing that everyone needs but that most people don't appreciate as much as they should: sleep. When my wife became pregnant, all my friends who were parents kept telling me, "Sleep—sleep all day if you can. Sleep any minute you get a chance, because once that baby comes, you won't be able to sleep anymore. Especially you, since you sleep in all day." Well, this might come as a surprise to them and maybe to you, since that is what most people believe promoters do all day, but for the past twenty years, I have been sleeping five to six hours on a regular basis. I was only able to get my full eight hours of sleep on Sunday mornings. Of course, most of my friends' memories are of trying to get in touch with me in the mornings, at ten or so, and me never answering their calls or telling them that I was asleep when they had been up for a few hours at work already. What most people consider normal is going to sleep around ten or eleven at night, sleeping their full eight hours, and waking up between six and seven to start their day bright and early. Not only is this a good amount of sleep for the average adult, but it is also the best time to do so, since it is during nighttime. Most people are asleep, so what are you going to do, being awake on your own? It is dark and quiet, which is perfect for sleeping like a baby. Also, due to some kind of energy that comes from the sun that does not allow you to sleep as well during the day, it is recommended that you avoid staying up at night and sleeping during daylight. The bad news for us in this business is that our sleep schedules must be the complete opposite of what is typical. If we wake up early, there is not really much for us to do, since most of the people we work with were up late the night before. Nightclub employees, managers, and owners don't go to the clubs until noon the next day and a lot of times even later. Nightclub-promoter meetings are usually held during evening hours on off nights. These are your Mondays through Wednesdays, usually between six and eight. That is the one area in my business that I was never very happy with, since I missed a lot of plans with my friends and clients during those morning hours, like going to pool parties. Going to the beach or on a boat was very hard for me because I was usually not ready in time. Only in my first five or six years as a promoter was I able to attend all these day events and still perform as well during the night. I started very early and was young, and therefore, it did not matter whether I went out on a boat straight after work; whether I had breakfast, took a shower, and went; or whether I just took a two-hour power nap. This is not something I can do today. I will elaborate on this matter more in chapter 3.

Another thing that you will have to give up on is going out where you please. If you want to be successful in this business, not only will you have to be at your own party every night that you open, but you will also need to check out the competition every chance you get. If there is a new club in town where everyone is going, but it has nothing to do with your niche and you will neither find new clients nor learn anything from their music or their entertainment or the way they work the door, then it is better that you use that time to go somewhere else where you will be able to actually do all these things. One more reason why you won't go to those places anyway is because if it is not in your niche, then they might not even know who you are, and if you are a promoter, you want to make sure that everywhere you go you are treated as such, meaning that you want to have the celebrity perks without having to be an actor or a band member. As you can imagine from what I said about the sleep, there is also a problem with your hours of operation. This will most likely cause you to have issues in your personal life with your family and friends, and even more with your significant others. That is why a lot of the people in the nightlife business end up dating others who either work with them or at least are colleagues that work in other bars or clubs, usually in the same niche as their own. In this field it is very hard to have a good, solid, serious relationship due to the nature of the business. I believe that this is the job with the second-highest rate of divorces after police officers, at least in the United States. Though definitely on a smaller scale than celebrities, promoters give up on their private lives. This is not as hard as celebrities have it, with paparazzi and all the gossip columns waiting for them to make a mistake so they can write about it, or to take a topless tanning picture so they can sell it to the highest bidder. But even if loss of private life is on a smaller scale for a promoter, it does affect your life and the things you do or not do in your local area. With all the social media and different nightlife picture-taking websites, promoters become local celebrities very quickly, so make sure to behave all the time, or they will find you. I know that this is not the case for all promoters, but it will be the case for you if you become the promoter that I believe you can be after reading this book and applying all the necessary techniques.

2

HOW TO BE THAT PERSON

Now that we have gone over a few of the negative sides of this beautiful business, there are only two possible scenarios. The first is that it scares you so much that you might not want to do this as a career anymore. Maybe you just want to do this as a hobby and promote as a part-time job. But most likely, if you picked up this book and are still reading it after all that, then it means you are interested in becoming a nightlife entrepreneur and want to make this a long, prosperous career. The first question you will have after making this decision is where to start. Universities or colleges will help you pursue certain careers. Not only do they teach you the step-by-step basics of any business you are planning on getting into, but they also introduce you to the field through internships that often earn you credit toward your diploma. But like I mentioned before, careers in nightlife entrepreneurship are not taught at the college level. I am working on making college studies in nightclub promotion a possibility for you in the future, and if that is the case by the time you read this book, then I strongly recommend that you go straight to the school that is offering this opportunity, look at its curriculum, compare it to everything you read here, and see if it is something that looks familiar. If by the time you finish the book you don't feel confident enough to start your career, then enroll in courses that focus on the areas you need more help in. If a college program is still not available in your city, what you should do is read this book chapter by chapter until you have what it takes and you know what it means to become a promoter or, better yet, a nightlife entrepreneur. On another note, make sure you understand that even if most of the time you will be getting paid to party, you are there to make sure others are having a good time. You don't always have to be having a good time, even though you have to look like you are and most of the time you will be anyway.

From my experience I can say that the average person between the ages of twenty-one and twenty-eight goes out two nights of the week. After age twenty-eight, people slow down and go out just once a week on average. When most people hit their midthirties, they go out only once a month, and even less in a lot of cases. Before the age of twenty-one is when people go out the most, which is mainly due to college and the fact that drinking is prohibited in most states. People tend to like the things that are forbidden. How much of your work will be actual partying for you really depends on your personality, how old you are, and where you are in life at the time you decide to start this business. Even if you are not a client but a promoter or a club owner, at some point in your career, it does not look good when a fifty-year-old man is drinking every night of the week. As a matter of fact, the more you can control the drinking, the better. It would be a lie if I said that in order to be a great promoter, you should not drink alcohol, but the truth is that while you are working, there is no job that allows you to get intoxicated. It may appear as if this one is different, but that is not the case. I will go into the truth about drinking as a promoter and how much is OK, in a later chapter.

Going back to what I was saying about how often the average person goes out during the week, remember that you will be going out as part of your work more than the average person. Just make sure you don't party like the average person, yet remember that you will always be the life of the party, if that makes any sense. A promoter by definition is a person in charge of marketing and promoting an event, venue, concert, or artist. There are sports promoters and concert promoters, and those professions are respected far more than nightclub promoter, but once in a while even those promoters wish they had our job. But what is promoting? Well, basically it is to encourage the sales, acceptance, or recognition of any of the above by the act of advertising or publicity. So in the definition alone of what promoting and a promoter are, we hear the words marketing, advertising, and publicity. This does not even mention the word entrepreneur, even though most nightclub promoters are self-employed and subcontracted. So if you need to be an entrepreneur who knows marketing, advertising, and publicity, why on earth would this not be considered a career? Well, I don't have the answer to that question, but I am hoping things will change sometime soon.

If you already know what it means to be a promoter, and you also know the cons of becoming one, then the next step is to figure out what type of promoter you are. Notice that I don't say what type of promoter you *will be.* This will be defined throughout your career, and there is no way of knowing now what you will become or how far you will go, although you can dream big and focus on your short- and long-term goals and thus accomplish all of your dreams in this career. But the main reason you don't know now is because I am pretty sure that these dreams will not only change, but they will also grow as your career in nightlife entrepreneurship starts to develop. The reason I ask what type of promoter you are is because I believe if you have gone this far, you already are a promoter. I know it because I once was you. I was dreaming of what I loved to do, and I saw all the great things you see about this business. Just make sure you know it too. More than anything in this world, a promoter needs to be confident, and the best way to be confident is to know your business like the back of your hand and to believe in what you are selling or advertising. That is why it is so important to know what type of promoter you are. Are you a nightclub or concert promoter? Do you want to promote bands or sporting events? Do you want to work part time or full time? Are you a majority or minority group promoter? All these questions will help you understand what you are going to do later. The hours you work as a concert or event promoter are different from those of a nightlife promoter. Therefore you need to know if you are a night owl or an early bird. Do you love music or sports, or maybe comedy? Even though promoting to Anglos in America might sound like you are promoting to a majority and a great idea, this is not the case when it comes to nightlife promotion. You need to define your niche even more specifically than that. For example, if most of your friends are white, what kind of music do they listen to? Is it heavy metal? Do they love hip-hop? Are they into house music? And even those categories can be further subdivided. The smaller the group, the better defined your niche will be. Remember, it is not only important to know what people around you like, but it is also important to know what you love. You will be the only person who attends 100 percent of all your events, so make sure you are not promoting a hip-hop event if you are into salsa. The bottom line in defining what type of promoter you are is knowing first if you are going into a different area of promotions or if you are still sure you like the nightlife as your future business. After that has been decided, you need to make sure you know if you are going to be a part-time subpromoter or if you are going to be a full-time nightlife entrepreneur. If the latter is your answer, then you make your first business decision as an entrepreneur: What is my niche?

In my case I was born in Barranquilla, Colombia, a small town with a big personality and big names like Shakira and Sofia Vergara. I moved from Barranquilla to Miami when I turned fourteen years old. At the time I was a very shy kid who had just been starting to make friends in my town, and now I had to start all over in a completely new world. My first trimester in Miami was hard for me because I was not so confident, with English being my second language and all, even though I had gone to the British American School my whole life. It took me a while to start making friends back then, but in a matter of three years, I went from being the shy kid sitting in the back of the classroom in eighth grade to this guy who in his junior year was dating a senior and who as a senior participated in every show possible, from acting to dancing and even civic acts. I loved being on stage so much that I would be part of the talent shows at my sister's high school too. At the time, my sister was a sophomore and president of her high school's Spanish club, which helped me a lot. Being part of all the shows that the Spanish club promoted made me more popular among the Hispanic community in both my high school and hers. I would say that 80 percent of my friends at the time were of Hispanic descent. With this said, it was obvious to me that I had to go into promoting for the Hispanic community if I wanted to be successful. Also, at the time that I started my promoting business, there was no other company or promoter working for this specific demographic. In Miami there are a lot of different groups of Hispanics, just like as I mentioned with Caucasians before. When I decided to start my business back in college, I was especially promoting to South Americans, everywhere from the northernmost spot in Colombia to the southernmost point in Argentina.

This brings me to the part of the story when my first partner, Victor, and I came up with the name for the company. If you are going to get into this business, it is very important that you open a company and choose a name for it. Most promoters think that it is about promoting their own name. Well, I am sorry to say it, but they are all wrong. This is a business, and you need to promote the business name like nothing else. This is called branding. Also notice that I mentioned a partner. I do strongly recommend that you do this business with someone else. Make sure that it is someone who is going to complement you. You and your partners will be the face of this company, and you all need to be on the same page at all times. When two heads are put together, they create a third fictional mind, which is the one that actually comes up with all the good ideas. Be humble and let that third mind get creative. It is very true that two heads are better than one, three are better than two, and so on.

Going back to the company name, make sure that you already know what your niche is, make sure you have an idea of what type of clubs you will be working with, and make sure you use a name that can be easily remembered, something that has a meaning, something fun. Like I said before, we were catering our events to a South American clientele. I can say that 95 percent of our clients and friends were from somewhere in South America. It was the first time in my life that I had been to an event where people from so many different countries were mixing and partying together without any issues. It was a beautiful sight. We started promoting these parties at a private clubhouse called Club de Cazadores. At the time we were having a party every two months, and by the third event, we were already drawing around two thousand people. Imagine the excitement when five nineteen-year-olds, with the help of a couple of subpromoters (mostly friends who didn't charge us), put together these three events that brought two thousand people together. We went with the high school idea of the open bar back then and made a deal with the clubhouse. We would pay them a $500 rental fee after the event, and in exchange we could use the place for forty-eight hours. We came in the day before to decorate a little and build the stage with our own hands and the hands of a lot of friends that got paid in beer. We also made a great deal with the closest local liquor store, which never even asked for ID when we ordered the amount of liquor we did. The deal was that we would get a truck delivered on consignment to the venue, and whatever was not used by us would be returned to them after the event. The bartenders, security, disc jockey, and all door staff also got paid after the event, so we basically opened the doors with no expenses. We were lucky that at the time nightclub flyers were not a big thing. We had a friend, Daniel, who would draw the design on a piece of paper, and we would make copies at Kinko's. We used the same type of paper all three times, and that actually taught me that repetition is very important. People associated the paper with a great party, and it gave brand recognition.

Well, the purpose of telling this story now is because after the third party, we decided to open our company and make it an official business. I knew that I loved to throw a party, that I loved to talk to people, that I loved to be the center of attention, and that nothing was better than seeing so many people have a good time all due to your own efforts. The only thing I was not ready for was the serious side of the business: a bank account, contracts, budgeting, and how much to invest. How much did we have, and what in the world was our name going to be? At the end of the third party, we sat down to count the money. With all the expenses being paid after, and with so many people showing up, it was a no-brainer that we were going to be rich so quickly. We were in for a huge surprise, as we finished counting the money very quickly. The first two parties had left us with enough money for us to pay for our food, buy a few clothes, and purchase the Kinko's copies that we needed for the third event. But this time we'd had more people than ever, and the money was not there. It did not make any sense. Where had the money gone? Had someone stolen it from us? Had we spent too much? Had we had fewer guests than we'd thought? Were people going in for free? We had never asked these questions before.

This was going to be our first rude awakening. We were starting to learn from our own mistakes. A couple of friends even said, "Maybe this is not such a good business after all." In the end, that was envy talking; they knew that we were the most popular kids in the city, at least when it came to our niche clientele. There was not one person between the ages of eighteen and twenty-one who had not been to our events or at least heard of them. At that time I made a decision: this was not going to end here. There were five of us throwing the party together, but only two of us were really serious about it as a business, Victor and I. I spoke to him on the side right after counting the money and said it was time to get serious. "Let's open a company," I said. "Let's do it!" He asked what we needed. All I remember was saying, "I'm not sure, but we need a name and a bank account for sure." Then another promoter friend walked in the room and asked, very surprised, "You guys lost money? How many people came? I saw everyone here." I answered in Spanish, "La misma gente de siempre," meaning "the same people as always." A second later I said to my partner, "That's it. That's the company name—La Misma Gente." He laughed and said, "Why not? I like it."

Two weeks later we were at the bank with our new company papers and our first loan—fifty dollars from my father, who was still not happy with the idea of me being a promoter and not an accountant, but in the back of his mind, I know he did believe. Twenty years later here we are with over fifty employees, and we are known as pioneers and the biggest nightlife entrepreneurship company in Miami that caters to the upscale Hispanic clientele. It is also good to remember that when you choose your company name, there should be a story behind it. In my case that is part of the story, but over the years I have been asked thousands of times where "the same people" came from. My story has always been the same, because it is real. Don't make up a story to build a name. The actual true story will remind you where you started and how much you have accomplished when you get here. I always say that we have two reasons for the company name. One is because the clients who go to our events are like a social club—they are always the same people, which is something people like, since people like to party with people they know. Only in Vegas will you hear a different story, since what happens there seems to stay there.

The other reason for our name is that with me being Colombian, my first partner being Venezuelan, and our clients being from Argentina, Chile, Peru, Uruguay, Paraguay, Ecuador, Bolivia, Panama, Brazil, and just about every country in Latin America, we also wanted to make it known that no matter where we come from, we are all the same people. Everyone seemed to like this story more than the first, so we stuck with that answer if it was a serious context like a radio interview or a story in the local newspaper.

The last thing you need to think about when coming up with the name are the possibilities for the name to evolve. In my case my company is no longer known as La Misma Gente, even though older clients from back in the day still call us that. We are known today as LMG, which has opened doors in different niches and is easier to remember. Also, when it comes to designing a logo, three letters are easier to work with than a long phrase.

This chapter is about how to become that guy, the promoter you see at the doors of the most prestigious nightclubs, the one that puts you on and off the list, the one who has the power to open the ropes (or at least you think he does), the one who comes outside and orders the doorman to open the door for the three beautiful ladies and for his two guy friends who are dressed no better than you, they just know him better than you do. We have talked about making the decision about what you are going to do, what type of promoter you want to be. We talked about going to school versus not going to school. Now you know what it means to be that guy. You probably already have an idea as to what your niche will be, at least at the beginning, and by now you might already be thinking of a few ideas about what to name your company. Maybe you even have a partner or partners in mind. This is great if that is your case; you have a head start and are probably going to be even more successful and faster than I was. This is always option one. But if that is not the case, do not get discouraged. Most people are not ready to start their own company from day one.

There are two other options that you can choose, and a lot less thinking goes into them. I suggest that you do either of them for a short period of time and work hard on getting the other two in order. Option two is becoming a direct employee of a nightclub and promoting for them. This is called an in-house promoter. A lot of nightclubs are looking for promoters who work on their own, but you can be sure that these won't be your A-list nightclubs where everyone wants to go. Those places usually open up with no promoters, and it is not until they realize that the nightlife is a promoter-driven business that they start calling the big promotional companies to work deals with them and expecting them to make the deals with all subpromoters. The bad thing about this is working different nights in the same venue, which is the hardest job.

This brings me to the third option, which is the one I recommend: working for a company like LMG. This gives you the opportunity to get into the best nightclubs in town right from the beginning. Even if the niche that LMG promotes is not your own, a company like ours has built a reputation over twenty years that opens doors for us to work at any venue to which we believe we can bring a strong clientele. If you believe you can do that, then it is our job as entrepreneurs to be able to read that from you. Working for a big promotional company gives you a lot of opportunities, since you can quickly grow within the company if you have it in you. Most promotional companies make the mistake of not helping the new up-and-coming subpromoters. This makes the subpromoters want to go on their own and use everything they have learned to turn into your most obnoxious competition. They will be calling your clients they met at your party and calling the club owners or managers you introduced them to. Two things are wrong about this. First, I think it's wrong to be the big company that does not give new promoters the opportunity to grow within the company. The way I see it, I want you to become the best promoter you can be to build your own business, but you need a partner. I am here to teach you everything you need to know in order to become a great promoter, and my door is always open. Maybe you'll realize that the expertise I have to offer and the new blood and energy you are bringing to the table are the perfect combination for a successful business.

The second thing that is wrong is for a promoter to work in any promotional company with the only purpose being to learn from them in order to later use that knowledge against them. Maybe you don't understand why I am talking about competition so early, but believe me, this business is a dog-eat-dog world. Everyone is on his or her own, unless you choose to do each and every step I will mention here. You need to be respected not only by clients and club owners, but mainly by other promoters who specialize or will be the future experts on your niche clientele. When I first started, there was a nightclub owner who thought that every time a new club opened, he would watch what they were doing. If they were not direct competition, he would leave them alone, but if they competed with him, then he made sure they did not make it—he put every effort into cutting their wings. The smaller they were, the more quickly he would destroy them with bigger, better, and much more expensive events or productions, and with ten times as much promotion. He wanted to make sure people knew who the big boy was and who the new kids were. He also said I should apply this strategy in my business, but I happen to disagree with the whole concept. I have done this a few times over the years, but only to those who decided that they were in any way going to take a share of my pie. I am willing to share the pie with everyone who wants to continue to grow with me, but if you are in this business to copy and overcome the ones that are already around, then I suggest you do it very carefully, because we are watching you. Just kidding—but don't do it.

So in conclusion, work for a nightclub, or work for a big promoter or company. It's better if it is a company; when someone is promoting only under their own name, you will only be building their name. Or start your own company and go all out if you believe you are ready. But my recommendation is that you work for a big, well-known company and show them what you are made of. Mention what your goals and plans are from the beginning. Don't be scared to ask for more when you believe you deserve more. We are very open minded when it comes to profit sharing, but not as much when promoters ask for salaries. Profit sharing makes a promoter work more than salary-based arrangements. Working for commission, as it were, is a big incentive, and it also makes you understand the value of the dollar by seeing how much money you can make but can also lose even if it first looks like you made a lot of money, like our third big event when we were getting started. Don't forget to ask for perks also. These are things like free drinks or complimentary bottles. The better you are, the more you get and the better you look to your clients.

If you choose to go on your own, you need to think about the next two steps, which are choosing the right venues and the nights you want to promote and then contracting your staff, if you bring your company to a club or bar. Since new companies start more with bars than actual nightclubs, make sure to bring all the staff you can, like doorman, guest list girl, cashier, DJ, and all entertainment. But if you are just getting started, the staff will probably be working for the club, since they will charge you as the amateur you still are. In this situation you need to get the best deal from the bar that you possibly can. Imagine this: you need to find a bar that needs help, but if they need help, it means people don't like going there in the first place, so why will your friends want to go there? Second of all you need to spend money on all your staff. To give you an idea, on average my company will open the doors of a bar with around $2,000 in expenses before the event even begins. Is this an overhead you want—are you willing to take that risk? (Don't run away now; I'll explain how you can lower or even eliminate the risk later on.)

Then there is the other side of working directly for a nightclub. I mean, yes, it could be the best club in town, and maybe all your friends will call you on Monday to make sure you've added them to the list. But be ready to hear a lot of complaints from these future ex-clients as soon as they arrive at the club and say your name to the doorman, who asked you not so politely to get back inside and then told your friends he did not know you, there is no such person working here. That is the biggest headache between promoters and doormen, and I don't believe there is a solution for it, unless you want them on your payroll, if you know what I mean.

Then there is the recommended option of working with a well-known promotion company. They will already have a club or a few clubs or even bars working on their main nights, sometimes even on the off nights. All you have to do is pick and choose which company best fits your niche.

Which of their clubs will work better for your schedule, and where can you bring more people with less effort? You will have no expenses, since this company should provide you with everything you need in order to promote your business and theirs. You need to understand from day one that you are their partner; that is why those companies take competition so seriously. It is just as bad as cheating on a significant other. Don't do it. Some companies like my own are even willing to start a new party simply based on a new promotional team that is willing to start from scratch but with access to all our resources. Also remember that just as with money, ask for what you want and need. If the company is successful, they will know if what you are asking for works, but even if they think it doesn't and you ask for it anyway, they know it might work for you, so why not try it again?

By this time you should know what it is that you want to do. And if you are still not committed to one decision, then read on as we talk a little more about the other reason you want to do this in the first place: money.

3

MONEY NEVER SLEEPS

I know now that in order to live a truly happy life, you need to choose a career not only that you are good at but that you enjoy doing. But even though doing what you love is the most important reason to pick a career, you know that most people, myself included, have something else in mind when deciding what to do in life, and that is money. When I was younger, I wanted to be a doctor, yet this desire was not based in any way on a dream of helping people or of finding the cure to a deadly disease or because I loved blood so much. As a matter of fact, at the first smell of an animal's open body in an anatomy class, I realized that this career was not for me. My career aspirations back then were based 100 percent on how much money doctors made. I wanted to make money to be able to buy more toys. And by toys I mean cars, boats, big houses, etc. It was not until the day that I sat with my counselor in college that I realized what I really loved doing.

Even though making the decision to become a promoter was based on what made me happy and what I loved to do every day, there was another big factor involved in my decision, and it was the cash. I had only done a few parties in high school without any study or any experience and had made a few easy bucks. Imagine how much money I was going to make if I made a career out of these experiences! Luckily, not only was I able to make it in this new career, which was not even considered a real job at the time, but I was also able to be very successful at it. I will not talk about exact numbers here because it is not polite, but I can say that I was the first of my friends to buy my own car, I was able to buy my first house at a very early age, and by the time I was supposed to be graduating from college, I was already making what would have taken me another eight years if I had been a doctor. Like any other entrepreneurial business, there are ups and downs, and the higher the risk, the bigger the reward. I have been doing this for twenty years now, and I have lost money on about 10 percent of our company's events. If you subtract that from the other 90 percent, it still leaves me with a very high profit margin. But this will only happen if you are smart with your numbers. The reason this chapter is called "Money Never Sleeps" is not because this is a nightlife entertainment business and therefore you make your money at night. "Money never sleeps" is a famous phrase from the movie *Wall Street*, and in that case it means that different world markets are open at different times. In this business you make your money at night and entertain your clients at night, but during the day, a lot of planning goes on. This is why you have to always be on top of your business, and even though the biggest, most important side of this business is the creative side, the other side, which is the accounting and budgeting and all the numbers in general, is the one that is going to help you make it or not in this business, and those transactions are handled during the day. Remember the third big event my company produced, where we had over two thousand people and did not make any profit? Well, that was my first real lesson in accounting and management. I cannot assure you that I did not make some of the mistakes twice, but I certainly didn't make them a third time.

This is also why I recommend that you do not drop out of school to get into this career, or any other for that matter. In the end any entrepreneur needs to know a little accounting and management skills. As long as you plan, organize, lead, and control your business, you will always be a step ahead of most promoters, mainly because most promoters tend to focus on the creative side only. Remember that you are going to be in the business of innovation. If you ask the average club owner the average life-span of a nightclub, you will get a different answer than if you asked most club goers, or at least the ones that set the trend. This is because a club owner will have different stages in his life cycle, while a client will be part of only one of those stages. We will not go over those stages now, since that is related more to the creative side of the business. This part of the business is the one activated by the other side of your brain, the logical side, the one that adds and subtracts and does not want to make small mistakes. Each one is just as important as the other. If being a promoter required going to school and getting a diploma or at least taking a small course on some of these things, I am sure there would be fewer promoters and more nightlife entrepreneurs. What is the difference, you ask? Well, the obvious one is the title alone. You will realize in your career that there will come a time when you will no longer want to be called a promoter. It was great when you were eighteen to twenty-two years old and all your friends would call you to make plans not only for the weekend but also on a daily basis. At that time in your life, being a promoter even makes you a leader by definition, if you are a good one, of course. People will follow you wherever you say they should go. You can be a really good promoter without ever learning any of the statistics, algebra, general math, and accounting concepts related to the business. You could probably even make some money if your people skills are just phenomenal. But without this financial part of the equation, you will never be considered more than that, a promoter, never a nightlife entrepreneur.

Another difference between promoter and nightlife entrepreneur is that a promoter has a shorter career life-span, at least in the nightlife business. On the other hand, a nightlife entrepreneur will live his full promoter life and then start his nightlife entrepreneur life as the former one ends or at least gets put on the back burner. It is kind of like comparing a major and a minor at your local university. In this case life is your only choice of university, at least until the right person picks up this book and realizes that this is something our society needs.

OK, so now that we understand the difference between a nightlife entrepreneur and a promoter, and we also understand the importance of the creative side as well as the business side or the logical side of the entrepreneur's mind, we can get started on what are those important things you need to learn. This is not a school textbook that is going to teach you actual mathematics equations, but I will share as much as I can about what has worked for most successful nightlife entrepreneurs like me during the past twenty years. Instead of you having to go through the trial-and-error process, I have done that for you and wish to help you start your new business with a head start over others who don't have this opportunity.

The first thing I have to say is that most promoters are very selfish when it comes to sharing—sharing clients, sharing ideas, sharing contacts, sharing plans that worked, and sharing secrets in general. I cannot say that it has been any different for me through my career as a promoter, but now that I consider myself to have graduated to nightlife entrepreneur, I understand that this is part of a process in life. Hopefully we will all reach a point in our lives and careers where we will share our knowledge. It could be with one person as a pupil, or we can share it with many, as I am today. The feeling of being able to help others do better by sharing your expertise is just incredible. This is something I have been doing little by little on a personal level with a few of my closest subpromoters, but it is not until now that I decided to make it as big as this book.

Getting back to business: What are the basic things you need to learn in this business in order to make it happen on the numbers and money side of the equation? Remember, this is a business of bringing people to places, and a lot of times you get paid according to the number of people you bring. This is called per head, and it has nothing to do with overhead. Overhead is the most important aspect of your business and anyone's business. Most people go into business without even understanding the concept of overhead. It is very simple. Overhead can also be called operating or fixed expenses. This probably sounds easier to remember, but you sound smarter if you know your overhead before starting any type of business. In the nightlife entertainment business, a lot of people think about their expenses as something that varies according to how the night goes. And this might even be true in some cases, or with some expenses like paying out subpromoters who get paid per head or a percentage of their table sales. But these are variable expenses that most of the time will not get you in trouble. As long as you have a good deal with your subpromoters, you will be OK. A good deal by definition means that both sides of the deal are satisfied with the equation. For example, if a subpromoter makes five dollars for each person he or she brings to the club, and you as a head promoter are in charge of paying the subpromoter, make sure that you are earning at least that same amount from the people he or she is bringing to your event. If you do, variable expenses will never subtract from your income; they will only add to your final profit.

When we talk about overhead, we mean the expenses that are fixed and happen on a regular basis in order for you to operate. Some examples of overhead expenses are a doorman, a DJ, flyer design, and printing, and in some cases these costs can be as much as office rent. The main idea is to keep operating expenses or overhead as low as possible without affecting the overall operations of the company. And get used to saying "the company," even if it is just you at the beginning. Make sure that your promotional company is always treated as a separate entity, as if it were another person you were talking about. As a matter of fact, a lot of people compare their companies to children. I cannot say that it is the same feeling, now that my child is on his way, but for the past twenty years, my company has been a top priority in my life. If I had ten dollars in my bank account and nothing else, I would give five to my company and five to myself. But if I had only one dollar, I would probably give it to my company first, because I am sure my company would be able to give me that dollar back with interest. In other words, treat your company as if it were your own child.

There is a theory I heard from my current partner, Gus, who heard it from his father. It says you need to take care of yourself first and then your company, because you are the backbone of your company. If you are doing well, your company will too. But since I am talking from my own experience, I can say that the higher the risk, the bigger the reward. I believed in my product so much that I always chose to take care of my company first, trusting that it would then take care of me. Both strategies might work, and maybe in the end, the final product is the same, but I cannot do it any other way because my business is what makes me who I am today. Come to think of it, I might even be the child in this relationship.

In order to keep the overhead low, the first advice I can give you is to shop around. When you are starting your promoting business and are contacting possible staff, you will be treated like a newbie. Everyone will try to get the most money out of you at first. Even though it is not recommended to do business with friends, I have my own theory when it comes to this type of business. You are going to need people you can trust almost in every position that might be contracted by you. And who can you trust more than your friends and family? When I am working at a nightclub, my job needs to be public relations. We as promoters are there to entertain and mingle with the regulars and new customers. But my money is being made at the door and the bars, so nothing makes me more at ease than to know that my wife is at the door and that someone else close to me is keeping track of the table and bar sales. Besides, everyone likes to party with friends, and like I said at the beginning, you need to make sure you are having a good time too. Keeping your friends close might be even easier if you give them a position. It is even better if they know that you trust them. Make sure they know that the reason they are there is because you trust them 100 percent.

Depending on the niche that you are going to work with, you also have to make sure the people working the door are the right fit for the crowd you will be inviting to your events. This might sound a little discriminatory, but looks are very important in this business, and you are not the only one who needs to take care of yourself. Your staff is going to be related to your company and your events, so it is very important that people have high praise for your staff. In most cases, when a promoter is starting in this business, he or she will not even be in charge of all these elements of the party. As a matter of fact, there are many promoters who never in their career end up in charge of expenses like the door staff or even the cashier. This is because they worked for another promotional company or directly for a nightclub, or simply did not understand the concept of having their own night, meaning that you make all the door money and some percentage of the bar in exchange for running the whole night. In my case this is how we started our business twenty years ago, and it is what we do best. Each time that someone else has been in charge of the nights that we have promoted, there have been issues. These issues go from something as small as a doorman who does not respect the promoter and his job to something as bad as a cashier taking money from the door that did not belong to her. Notice I say "her." I do recommend that cashiers be ladies in this business, since most of the clients paying a cover will be guys, and they are a bit more ashamed to ask for discounts when a lady is at the door. The same concept applies to a waitress versus a waiter. There are some very good waiters out there, but 95 percent of the best servers will be ladies—or at least they will sell more. But that really won't apply to you; most of the time, the bar and table services will come directly from club and bar owners themselves. But occasionally you might run into a venue that needs more help with its operations than you would think. Every time you get a chance to step in and recommend a staff member, it's a good opportunity, so take it. The more people you have on the inside, the more comfortable you will feel at this venue, and this might mean a longer life-span in the long run.

You will find expense sheets in Excel format on my website, *The Nightlife Entrepreneur*, link https://thenightlifeentrepreneur.com/, where you can download them and make changes as you wish. If you start as a subpromoter, make sure you have no expenses whatsoever. The company or club you are working for should provide all materials for your promotions, including business cards, flyers with your name, VIP cards with your name and number, and any other promotional material they might use. The only expense that you should have is gas and drinks that you might want to buy for possible new clients. This investment will come back very quickly. Sooner than later you will also start making new acquaintances at other bars, like bartenders and servers, so you might get some comp drinks as they start to get to know you as a colleague. This is another reason why I recommend that you start working for a promotion company that provides all this material instead of starting with an overhead from day one.

If you are already at a stage where you have worked for a promotion company or nightclub but are ready to take the next step, then these are a few of the expenses you will need to spend on, but take care that you're not paying too much. Let's start with the doorman. Make sure this is someone who has done this job before or at least someone who dresses well and has people skills. It is also important that this person knows your clientele. Even though a doorman may become a promoter, it is never good to mix these two. If a doorman is a promoter himself, there will always be a conflict of interest between him and your other promoters or subpromoters, since he has the benefit of being at the door and talking to every single customer. Besides that, the doorman is the one who decides who gets in and who does not. He is the one responsible for the type of people you have inside your venue. No matter how much you try to tell subpromoters not to invite a certain type of crowd to your events, they will always try to get as many people in as possible. Remember, they make money per head, so the more the merrier, as far as they're concerned. Unless that is the case for your event, be concerned about quality, and make sure your doorman is being extra careful at the door. So pick well. He is also the first person people will deal with and see when arriving to your party.

Then comes the cashier. I mentioned it before, and I will mention it many times in this book: the cashier is the person you need to trust the most. This person is handling your money. If your doorman decides who gets in, your cashier decides who pays and who doesn't. Just like everyone else at the door, this person needs to dress and look the part. There is a third position that is needed most of the time, unless you have a small party, and in that case, the cashier can do both of these jobs. This is the guest list girl. Back in the day, the guest list was an actual list of guests who you invited to a nightclub or event. It was in alphabetical order, and it could be anywhere from one page to as many as twenty pages. The guest list's only purpose was to indicate who had to pay and who did not. In today's nightlife, the guest list girl has become what we call the tally girl. This is someone who has taken over all other positions in importance. I am happy to say that my wife is currently my tally girl, and a very good one at that. Like the doorman and cashier, the tally girl needs to look good at all times. Lucky for me, I have a beautiful wife—perks that come with the job. If you keep this person next to the cashier, she will now be the one who actually makes the decision about who pays. A lot of nightclubs keep the tally girl next to the doorman. I prefer my tally next to the cashier, because that way I do not need to use the ticket system, in which each client at the door gets a ticket in one of three different colors, and the color determines what cover they will be charged. When the tally is the person you trust the most out of the whole door crew, you put that person next to the cashier and make sure she is the one making the decisions. This also makes the process faster, since clients don't have to be asked twice if they are with a promoter.

These three staff members—doorman, cashier, and tally girl—are the first ones you must have if you plan on starting your business. On the Excel sheets I have included in my website, you will see a lot more expenses, but these will all depend on your negotiation with the venue and how advanced you are in the production side of the business. I like to be in complete control of the night, but that can be difficult for a new company, since it takes a lot of time away from the promotion. To give you a better idea, in one of our nightclubs today, I pay the following staff members from my part of the cut: doorman, bottle-service man, tally girl, cashier, hostess for record keeping, database girl who collects information from clients, disc jockey, entertainers, subpromoters, flyer designers, flyer printers, street team, social media advertisers, and photographer. All of these are expenses for the night alone. Then I have my fixed operating expenses of office and accounting, which are a lot of overhead.

The last things I will be talking about in this chapter are club deals. This is a shark-eat-shark business. Unlike other businesses, where there are fixed fees and preset percentages for different types of relationships, in this business you could be doing the same exact job that someone else is doing for one-tenth of the money they are making. Since my partners and I were pioneers in this business, we had no basic information when we started that we would discuss with club owners. For example, most promoters in Miami today are working deals that make them a profit from both the door and the bar sales. This is something that has been learned through the years, and a lot of us old promoters learned the hard way the difference between a good and a bad deal (a good deal is when both sides are happy). As a matter of fact, when we started in this business, we did not make any money on the bar sales. This was very hard to accept after doing some events outside of nightclubs where 100 percent of the bar sales were our own. The difference between those events and the nightclubs was the repetition. Those were events that we had every three months, while the nightclubs were on a weekly basis.

The percentage of door sales and bar sales is going to change depending on a few different factors. The first is your background: Are you new in the business? Are you a well-known promoter? Are you a well-known company? How many years have you been doing this, and have you been successful? Do you have any references? If you do have them, use the ones that have the best things to say about your performance and that of your team. Some promoters go into nightclubs looking for fixed salaries. This is the first bad sign in this business. A well-trained business owner should know that a promoter who is asking for a fixed salary is most likely not going to perform well. It is better that everyone be partners for the night. This way, if one does well, so does the other.

Your deal with a club may change depending on what you will be doing for this venue. In my case we look for nightclubs that want us to do as much work as possible. For example, we promote, but we also produce the events. We look for the DJ, the artist, the performers, the door staff, and even bar staff if needed. When we do all this work, we ask for 100 percent of the door and 20 percent of the bar sales. Having been on the other side of the business as a nightclub owner in two different countries, we learned very quickly that there is a certain percent that we can give a promoter from the total bar sales. If any owner offers you more than 20 percent of bar sales, it's a red flag. Make sure to ask around if he owes any money before you sign that contract. That is as bad a sign as a promoter having a fixed fee. The reason why this is bad is because a nightclub has a lot of expenses that people don't see, and after all these expenses are paid, there is a certain percentage of sales left over for the owners. This percentage should vary in a good nightclub, between 25 and 30 percent, so if an owner is giving you everything that is left, it does not make any sense. Either the owner is not good with numbers, or he just won't pay you. Also, let's say you run into a nightclub that is used to making 30 percent profit from its sales. If you take more than half of that, they might not be so happy. Remember, both parties have to make money and like the deal.

I start all my deals with a three-month trial period. After that, I can either be let go, or I can quit if it is not working. But the most important aspect is that the deal can be fixed depending on what is going on those first months. Less than three months is probably not enough time to know if the deal is good. I have had parties where we hosted over a thousand people, with a cover charge of twenty dollars, a bar that sold more than forty tables at $500 each, and bar sales of another $20,000, and I still went home with no money. But there have been parties where I hosted four hundred people, with almost no cover and bar sales of $18,000, and I made a good week's pay. The reason why this happens is the deal. The two factors that affect the deal are the base deal and the splits from the door and bar. The best option for a well-known promoter should be 100 percent of the door and 20 percent of the bar. But even with that perfect deal, you can lose money if another part of the deal is that you pay all the expenses. So make sure you keep as many expenses as possible on the owner's side, because he or she gets most of the pie. But also keep people you trust on your payroll. For example, if it is your door, you should pay the cashier. But a DJ, even if he is your employee, should be kept on the nightclub's side of the equation.

On the spreadsheets in this chapter, you can see what kind of expenses should be on your side, depending on your deal and also on the size of the venue and its capacity. Here is a quick equation or way of seeing the monetary value of a good deal. Your door should account for about 10 percent of your total bar sales. So if you make $3,000 at the door, you should sell $30,000 at the bar. With that said, you make 100 percent of the door ($3,000) and 20 percent of the bar ($6,000), the club keeps 80 percent of the bar ($24,000), and everyone is happy. Keep those expenses low and most of the $9,000 will go to you in one night alone. Work three good nights a week and voila! The capacity factor is also one to consider, unless you will be a very upscale promoter. The reason is because the difference between quality and quantity is huge when it comes to promotion. The smaller your niche, the easier it will be to fill that niche with upscale

4

SIZE MATTERS

In chapter 1 I told you the story about how I was going to school to study accounting, and even though it did not turn out to be a career that made me happy, it still has become a big part of my success in this business. At the very beginning of my studies, I learned a basic accounting equation that in the end sums up the most important reason why you learn accounting in the first place. This equation, which has stuck with me, helping me manage my company and my personal expenditures, is *assets equal liabilities plus capital or owner's equity ($A=L+C$)*. At the time that I learned this equation, I was still studying accounting for beginners in high school, and the equation was so easy to remember that it helped me through my short accounting career. I did not know at the time how important it would be in my near future. Although I am not going to bore you in this chapter with mathematical equations or anything like that, I still want you to understand the value and meaning of this simple concept and to apply it to your new business. I will also tell you what your most important asset is or will be.

OK, let's start by understanding the basics of the equation. What are assets, what are liabilities, and what is capital? The simplest way to put this is that an asset is what is yours—what you have, what you own. This includes your cash, bank account, and any furniture or tangibles. A liability is what you don't have or what you owe. And capital is money that you and your partners invest in your company, plus any profits the company earns. I guess it is not as simple as that, but for our purposes it will work, and in the end that is what will matter. If you understand this equation in that way and you are always aware of it, you will know how much you can spend, what you can't purchase, what you should buy or sell, and so on. Liabilities are debts that you have to pay, and the only other way to get rid of a debt is to go bankrupt or not pay it. Neither option is a good one if you want to keep the business running and maintain a good reputation. The investment you put into your company will never be the same for everyone. It really depends on what your possibilities are, what kind of investors you have, if any, and whether you have already saved up money or have a loan from your friends or family. It is not easy to get a loan for this type of business from a financial institution. Banks consider us high risk, so I would not waste time on that route. (This is another good reason why there should be more education available for our line of business.) The money the company makes will also vary depending on the types of events you hold, the number of people who attend, and the number of clubs or venues you run. Watch out for this part of the equation, because sometimes less is more. Don't think that at the beginning of your career, opening three clubs a week is an easy task. You might end up losing in one night what you made the rest of the week, so be careful at first. Start small and grow slow.

What if I told you that your assets could change in value? In accounting that is called depreciation (losing value) or appreciation (gaining value). For example, let's say that you buy twelve water guns for your summer pool parties. You spend twenty dollars on each of those guns. These guns will depreciate in value every time they are used. Now let's say that the following year you decide to do these parties again, and now a bigger, better, nicer gun is on the market. The smartest thing to do is to sell the old guns. Using the Internet is the easiest way, through eBay, Craigslist, or one of the new apps that help you sell anything. If you sell those used guns for five dollars each, explaining that they were only used a couple of times, look like new, and are in good condition, you will still get back sixty dollars from the $240 that you spent. This means that the value of that asset went down $180. Not many assets have the possibility of appreciating in value, except for the ones that are intangible. For example, your reputation is an asset that could appreciate in value. It is impossible to put a price on your reputation, but it can certainly get worse or get better. The longer you are in business, the most likely that your reputation has become better; otherwise you wouldn't be around. These intangible assets are also very important for your business, but they have no monetary value, unless you are selling your business and have to put a price on every little thing.

Now that you know what your assets, liabilities, and capital are, let's talk about the one asset that can not only increase in value at the time of a sale of the company but that can also increase in value as you operate your company. Is it tangible or intangible? Well, there is no real price or market value for it, so that would make it intangible. However, you can actually touch it, so that would make it tangible. Mine actually has grown so much over the years that it has gone from free to not for sale. I actually rent or lease this asset, which makes me a profit for the company and grows my capital, therefore growing my assets. Remember, your capital grows your assets, and your liabilities lower them. I wonder if you already know what I am talking about. Let's see: it's not for sale but can be rented; it has no market value; it has a price you determine, and people that want it decide if they want to pay for it; you use it every week, but it does not wear down; it does not depreciate in value unless you sell it. Many will tell you that the quality is the most important part, but I will say that size does matter. Size is what most people will pay for. But I have to be honest and say that if you want to rent it more than one time to the same client, you need to make sure that quality is also good. The way to make sure that quality is good is to be organized and keep it clean and easy to use. I could keep giving you hints about what it is, but I am not going to keep you waiting any longer. (Did I say longer? Ha!) The most valuable asset, one without a price but worth every penny, is your customer database. Some call it the guest list, some call it client list. In the end it is your most valuable data.

There are different types of data that are important to your company and its value. For example, there is data that keeps track of all sales and events you have done in the past. This data is very important to you, but not as much to the company. Your customer database is as important as all other assets put together. If we were to close the company today, after twenty years of hard work, keeping a good reputation, paying everyone on time, paying every penny owed to everyone, keeping a great relationship with all club owners and managers, and maintaining a good relationship with subpromoters and even sometimes with the competition, as crazy as that may sound, we would lose a lot of power if we wanted to get started again. Building a name or brand is hard work, and twenty years of that is hard to get back. But with the power of that database, you can always start fresh. It would not take me another twenty years to achieve the same status the company already has. Most people I would work with would already know who I am, and if they didn't, they might have heard of my company, so I could use the name to introduce myself. When informing people of your new events with your new company, there is nothing more powerful than going straight to those who have been your clients in the past. Try using designs that look like your old one; use personal names once in a while to remind people who you are or to inform them that it is you with a new company name.

On the other hand, imagine how hard it would be the other way around. Let's say you have twenty years working with your company, but you lose your database. Imagine opening a new party then. How will you let all your customers know that this is your new venue, what night it is, or when is it opening? This is all very easy with a well-kept database but near impossible without one. This is also a reason why I recommend you start your career with a company like mine—so you get to use our data. Unless you want to start from zero every time, make sure you keep this information as safe and organized as possible. And when I say safe, I mean *safe*. I have had so many issues with my database in the past that today I understand its value and prefer to keep it myself in such a safe place that I will not even mention it here. You never know who might pick up this book.

Going back a bit to the subject of quality versus quantity, which I mentioned at the beginning of this chapter, there is a reason why I say that quantity is the most important part but that you cannot build a large database without hosting big events and having a couple of years of experience in nightlife promotion. On the other hand, it's better to build the quality of the database from the moment it is started. For example, let's say this is going to be your first event ever, and you expect a reasonable turnout. Make sure that you store this information and keep it very well organized from day one. This information should include things like name, phone number, e-mail, and home address, even though the physical address is slowly being forgotten. But in the end, the most important information will be that which defines your clientele; it is what will separate them from any other simple database. It is what will define your database as being part of a specific niche. For example, you can add gender, and you can add nationality if it is important to you. You can add age (or age group so you don't offend anyone). You can also add a space for ethnicity or the type of music they like the most. All of these factors make your database better organized and easier to use in the future. You do not want to waste money sending information about a hip-hop concert to your entire list when you have clients that only listen to Spanish rock. Another reason why you want to make sure that your client list is well organized and differentiated is because when it comes to selling it, you will have the edge over the other company who simply has a lot of names that one can easily find in a phone book or on Facebook.

Another very important piece of information is the client's household income. This is information that you do not want to ask for the first time your client comes to your event. The less information you ask from your clients at the beginning, the fewer complaints you will get. Remember, they are here to have a good time, and collecting their information takes time away from their night, so make this experience as easy as possible. For example, get a good-looking, outgoing woman to be the one who collects data from your patrons. Make sure she is always smiling and that she is dressed according to the venue and event. A big plus for the data collector is if she gives something away. This is really going to depend on the freedom you have as a promoter with the venue or if you are sharing this information with the venue. This way they gain more and are willing to give more out. It also depends on how deep their pockets are, and yours. Let me give you one scenario with the database collector. Let's say she tells each client that they will be part of raffle that will take place in the middle of the night. The winner will receive a complimentary table with no cover at the door for the following weekend, a prize valued at x dollars. I have found that when people are going to give you something, they expect something in return. In this case, people are more willing to give complete and correct information, because they want to win and don't want problems when they try to cash in their prize. On a bigger scale, if your venue or club owner has deeper pockets, you might convince them to give a complimentary drink or glass of champagne to those who fill out the information sheet. If this is the case, make sure you get a little more information, since the average price for a drink is going to be about what an average person makes in an hour at a regular nine-to-five job. Make them work a little for their drink; they will still fill the information out.

One of the biggest issues with collecting data at a club is that people are drinking and are not in the mood to fill out papers or stop their partying for your business. There are two steps that make this easier and also make the database more valuable. The first is to make sure that the girl who is collecting the data is the same person who is recording the information on a sheet of paper or an iPad. The second thing that helps a lot is, if you send each client some kind of confirmation code for their prices. Let's say that Juan is at the club and wants to get that complimentary drink. He thinks that he can come and give you fake information and still get that drink ticket for his comp at the bar. To get his real information, tell him that in order to get the free drink, he will need two passwords, one of which will be sent to his e-mail and the other texted to his phone number. He must present both to the data collector or bartender if he wants to get his drink. This way you get the correct information every time, and you make sure that people are not getting drinks more than once. I'm sure you will have other ideas about how to get this done without all this trouble, but this is just an example.

When it comes to the size of the database, there is an issue that I always seem to run into nowadays, and this is due to so many people offering promotional services and not delivering. This is a situation that has happened many times in the past, and it most likely will happen again. When it comes to selling services, I have always been the type of person to believe that it is always better to underpromise and overdeliver than the other way around. There is nothing worse than making the club owners or managers get ready for a huge night, only to have them overstaffed or end up with a bunch of liquor that they won't get rid of. The first impression is always the most important, and this applies not only to the way you should look when you come to offer your promotional services, but especially to the first night. Managers, owners, and staff in general will remember this first night like no other. When you are starting in this business, you might not be capable of packing a nightclub on your own, or you might not be able to sell out your first show or concert. If you already know that this is the case with you and your company, make sure that you don't promise that it will happen anyway. As your company grows and your database starts to build up, however, you need to start measuring the number of people who are coming to your opening nights every time you start a new venture. There is going to come a day where you need to promise exactly what the club is going to get, but make sure they believe you. Try to get inside information from staff members before opening. They can always tell you what owners and managers are saying about the new party that is coming, how many staff are on the schedule and starting at what time, and so forth.

A few years ago, we did the grand opening for a nightclub that had closed its doors two years before and had just reopened under new management. We decided to give this venue a try, since it had been so successful for us in the past. The whole time that we were negotiating with the new management and ownership, we talked about our expectations and about how we knew we had done there in the past and thus were sure we would be sold out from day one. We even went as far as sending them some staff that we knew were great at handling our clientele so that we did not have to worry as much about service. Everyone was so pumped. This was going to be such a perfect opening—packed, great service, great music, nothing to worry about, and people would come back the second week without thinking about it twice. We even had backup plans, with a list of events ready for the venue every week for the first two months. To make the story short, what I can tell you is that we had over a thousand people, which was the capacity for this venue. The music was a little off, but that was fixed as the night went on, and that is our job. We expected a certain clientele, but a younger demographic showed up, which made the music very different, believe it or not. But the main issue was the service. There were a total of five waitresses, one barback/busser, and four bartenders in a nightclub that had four bars, forty tables, and hosted a thousand patrons at once. It was simply impossible for us to come back from that disaster of a night after the horrible comments people were making on the street. One person said he arrived at eleven o'clock and wasn't seated until one in the morning. He still stayed and consumed alcohol, but when he asked for his tab, he waited another hour before he got it and could leave. In addition, the liquor on the menu was not the liquor in stock, and the prices in the computers were not the same as the prices on the menus. The servers did not even know the manager when they came in to work—everyone met each other that same night. There was nothing else we could do that night but drink with our friends and make the best of it.

I am at a point today where the percentage of the crowd that I know from my database and my parties has gone way down. But back when we started the company, we probably knew 95 percent of the clients that attended our events. I'm talking about parties with around 1,000 people where we personally knew 950 of them. As crazy as that sounds, that was the case. Yes, there was less competition back then, if any, but it was still a round-the-clock job. We were going out every day of the week during the day to malls and restaurants, passing out business cards and flyers, taking phone numbers, giving VIP cards to potential new clients, inviting people to lunch, and exchanging VIP cards for other types of services like laundry and car washes. You have no idea how powerful those VIP cards were back then. Remember that this small piece of cardboard or paper that may cost you little or nothing has value for all customers who don't get to be on the guest list or who have to get in line and pay a cover at a club.

The problem nowadays is that at every club in the city, everyone knows someone who knows someone who called himself a promoter. That is one of the main problems that I am looking to fix with this book: not only educating those who are interested in making this a business, but keeping those who destroy the business away from our bread and butter. The reason why today I only know about 5 percent of my database or clientele that actually go to my parties is because most of the clients that I have personally known or called my friends have done something they call growing up. This is something that I was not ready to do as a promoter, but it happened when I became a nightlife entrepreneur. Most of my original clients have met someone special and gotten engaged or married, had children, or joined a religion that does not permit them to drink alcohol. Although they all come back at some point in time, the core of the business today is a new, younger demographic. When I say younger, I mean they are younger than my original clients are now, of course, but they are probably in the same age group as my clients were when I started in the business. The other night I got a call from a good friend in the middle of the night on a Saturday. When I picked up the phone, he asked, "Are you at the club?" and I said, "Of course." He then asked if I was at the front door, which I was, so I said, "Yes, yes, I'll come get you." To my surprise his answer was, "No, I'm not there, it's my son with some friends. Make sure they don't wait too long." True story. Some might think that this is depressing, yet I think I have accomplished something that most can't in this or any other business. We have been around for two decades and expect to stay for another one coming. Even though I am getting close to my forties and having my first child, every time I run into high-school friends who have nine-to-five jobs or simply work in a different type of business that is not related to entertainment, I seem to be the one who feels the youngest. Yes, they might have done some things that I have not done yet, like changing diapers and getting puked on (actually that did happen to me, but that story goes in the next book). But even taking that into consideration, I still feel younger than my age.

Getting back to the reason why I know fewer of my clients today than I did back then: the second reason, aside from my clients getting older, is the fact that the newer, younger clients need new subpromoters to take care of them and host them in my events. There is one thing that age does affect in this business, and that is the hosting and actual inviting process. Unless you want to start working for an older crowd and events that still cater to your older clientele, then you have to open up to the possibility of starting a team of younger promoters who have all the qualities you first saw in yourself. Today, it is most likely that you are reading this book because you are still at that level where you are the new young promoter. Perhaps an older, more experienced nightlife entrepreneur like me dragged you into this business or saw a future in it for you. I would say that about 80 percent of subpromoters stay at that level for the duration of their career, which usually lasts about four years, the same time they spend going to school. Those guys take this as a part-time gig and never discover their full potential or don't ever understand the possibilities in this business. Customer relations are so important in maintaining a valuable database and clientele. This is why no one will do this job better than you yourself. But when the time comes to step out and allow the younger generation handle the day-to-day conversations and invitations of your new customers, you will understand it is the right time. There is no set date, age, or time for this; it is probably different for every person. I went into this business thinking I would be in it for a very long time, maybe ten years. Never did I believe that there would be a way for me to still be around and at the peak of my career twenty years later.

The best way to keep your client list growing is to use all your personal relationship skills—your charm, your connections. Treat everyone like your best friend. Don't do to others what you don't want done to you. Dedicate time to as many people as possible. You will always have a group of friends who will be your best friends. Mine have been around for the past twenty years or more. Some have worked with me, and some have only been clients for a while. But these are the guys or girls that you bring home almost every day. Don't ever be afraid to introduce them to all your new friends. You never know which of your friends will be the one to help you later in promoting your parties for free. Remember that word of mouth is a very powerful way of getting people back to your venues. The better they feel treated by you and your friends, the more they will help.

It is also very important to always network and keep business cards on you. The more people who have your information, the easier it will be for them to locate you and for you to keep them informed. But even more important than giving them your info is making sure you get their information too. Then every time you get a chance, go back into your database and add these new names and numbers. Every time you get a chance, speak to a possible new client or a client who is already at your event but whom you don't know well. Ask that person about his or her life; do not make it all about you. Promoters seem to be very outgoing—we like talking, we like being the center of attention, and though we don't realize it, we may talk more than we think, and more than one person may not like that. Everyone needs to feel important, and the best way is to include him or her in the conversation and to make sure you listen. Nothing is better than calling someone by his or her first name or asking about a personal matter next time you see that person. Save names on your phone, with hints to remember who these people are. Make sure these are good hints—don't just note the place where you met them or the drink they had; make it something that you will always remember. You have to treat everyone as equals; you never know who you are talking to. For some reason the people who show off the most seem to be the ones with the least possibility of being a good client. But one person is everything, so make sure that you treat each and every one as your best client or friend. Come by his or her table from time to time, bring over friends and introduce them, and make sure he or she is having a good time. that person will never forget this. You would think that it happens all the time, but it is less common every day. The only people mingling with clients lately are the servers, and this is not good for the business. They end up taking your clients wherever they go to work. You need to make sure that you are doing it, or at least that one of your subpromoters is. Also, take care of the servers and barbacks—they will help you out.

Remember that this chapter is all about the size. Yes, it does matter. Do not let anyone tell you otherwise. Those who say size does not matter just don't have it. Grow that database, grow followers, and grow fans, raving fans. Grow promoters and subpromoters. Grow your phone book.

5

IT'S ALL ABOUT THE SHOW

We are almost halfway through this book, and you should be well on your way to understanding what it is that you should be doing if you want to be successful in this business. But you probably still don't have a clue as to specifics on how you should do them. You already know that this is a career and not a hobby; you understand what you need to do today in order to get started on this amazing journey; you have a basic understanding of the importance of managing your money in this as well as any other business; and last but not least, you know that, as in other aspects of your life, size matters. Hopefully by now you understand what I'm talking about when I say size matters. But in case you don't, remember, I am talking about your guest list, your database, your client base, your patrons—everyone who works with you and/or has attended at least one of your events in the past. The bigger, the better.

In this chapter we are going to talk about one of the most fun parts of the job: the show, the party, the event, the night of. Whatever you might like to call it, in the end it is the few hours of this job when everyone else gets to have fun and you get to look like you are having fun too. This is the reason why everyone else wants to be in your shoes. They want to be on the other side of that rope. They want to go backstage. They want to jump in the bar. They want to be seen with all those gorgeous girls at their table. They also would love the free booze and complimentary admission that comes as an almost mandatory benefit at any venue in your city. That's if you make it. But don't worry, you will. You got started in the right place. You know when people say, "I wish I could go back in time to my high-school years with all the knowledge I have today"? Well, this is the way I feel today writing this words. I wish someone would have taken the time to hand me this book back then, or that I had had the opportunity to learn all I have learned on the street in an educational institution instead. I was one of the few lucky ones who did it at the right place, at the right time, and for the right niche. But I did not know it would be this good and last this long. On the other hand, there is a great feeling in writing this and knowing that people like you will make their living in this business, have a fun and happy life, and be able to do it because of these words, combined with their own personal effort.

The first thing that I am going to talk about in this chapter is being organized. Yes, it is that simple, yet it is so important. The first few years of my nightlife career, I was very disorganized, and I paid the price not once but many times till I learned the hard way that I had to change in order to stay competitive, to stay innovative, to save money or spend it well, and to make it in this fast-growing business. There are many aspects of this business that work better if they are well organized. Since we have been talking about the database and how its size matters, let's start with that. I cannot sit here and say that if you come to me with a database of fifty thousand people in a certain area of the city who have attended your events, I am not going to be interested in it. That has a value for sure. But if you came to me with that same database and told me that you have men and women separated, that you know these people's incomes, nationalities, and ages, and that you even have them separated as regulars and VIPs, you've just multiplied the value of that database exponentially. And if I am interested in it, don't think for a second that others will not be. I am not even talking about your competitors. I am talking about local businesses, and I am talking about big brands. Let's say that you go to a big brand. Imagine that a certain car company has a new car that is perfect for a young demographic, and they are looking to promote this car within the Hispanic community in your area. This just so happens to be your niche, and your database is divided and well organized. The car company might be interested in using it, and there are different ways you can offer it to them. You could charge them to send it out once as an e-mail blast. You could sell it to them for a higher price—not something I recommend, but you could if you decided to do so. You could offer to let them do an event with you at one of your concerts or venues. This is my favorite option because they become your sponsor. This gives you a lot more credibility, gets you on the map with other possible sponsors, and opens doors to other venues that might want those brands associated with them. The other good thing is that the company will help you build the show for that specific night. There are fifty-two weeks in the calendar year, meaning that you have 52 events a year if you have one night at one venue, 104 events if you have two nights, 156 if you have three nights, and so on. The perfect equation for a big promoter or a company is to have three nights. Depending on your niche, you would then pick which nights are better. In my specific niche, the best days for me to manage are Thursdays, Fridays, and Saturdays. This means we have a minimum of 156 events a year. Then you add the big special events and concerts that we do elsewhere, as well as the corporate and private events that we started doing over a year ago, although that is considered a different business, even though it came from being organized in this one.

The most common sponsors in this business are liquor companies, for obvious reasons, but I do recommend that you dedicate most of your time to different types of businesses. The main reason is because most liquor companies like to do business with the person in charge of buying from them—in this case, the nightclubs. Unless you are planning to buy your own venue, then look for sponsors in other areas. The other reason to seek out sponsors other than liquor companies is because they are helping less and less every day. Back when we started, we had liquor companies giving us checks for $5,000 plus free liquor and promotional materials; some would pay even more to be exclusive. But for the past few years, liquor companies have only been helping with free booze in exchange for a big purchase from their distributors, or sometimes not even that, and all they do is a buyback, which is a small purchase from your bar that they give out to your clients for free. This is not very rewarding for you because the liquor they buy is what they end up giving back to those clients who will not spend that money on your bar anymore, so it is not a win-win situation.

Another list that must be well kept and organized is the list of vendors, also known as providers. This includes everyone from a subpromoter to a big international band manager and everything in between. Without this list, you will always find yourself asking other people to make calls for you. You will even forget that you have met certain people who might not be big today, but you never know where they will be tomorrow. That's another reason to treat everyone as a VIP. I remember a few years ago, we had a client named Armando. Most people had no idea who he was, including me, but a few waitresses would treat him really well because he was a good tipper, and he seemed to be very nice to the staff. He would come in and sit in a corner at the main bar, have a few drinks, and go home. One of my subpromoters who is very good with public relations (PR) decided to go hang out with this guy and invite him a couple of drinks one night. They exchanged numbers and became friends just like that. Today this guy is no longer known as Armando; he has a couple of names. In Miami he is known as Pit Bull or Mr. 305, and in the rest of the world, he is known as Mr. Worldwide. We have had the pleasure of having him at our events, which is a very big deal in this city. Just having him there actually makes the whole show better.

So, make sure to keep all contacts in order, remember faces, save the numbers with pictures, and write a note to help you remember who everyone is—believe me, you will need it. I have about twenty different Carloses in my phone book. Another reason to keep these numbers is that you never know when you might need an emergency save from one or more of these providers, even if they are not your regulars. Anything is possible, and the show must go on. One night my main DJ for the past twenty years, DJ Willy, fell asleep at the wheel on the way to our party. We did not even know what happened till the next day, but a half hour into the time that we were supposed to open, we decided to call another DJ, who was not as popular, to take over Willy's spot for the night. Thank God that nobody knew this kid and he had no other gig that night. He did a spectacular job and saved the night. This kid has now been halfway around the world playing in different clubs and festivals, and we can say that we gave him his first opportunity. It is a great feeling being able to help others achieve their dreams, and in this case it was due to keeping our contacts well organized.

This is especially important when we are talking about the heart of the party—nothing is more important than music. This is what makes people have a good time, remember the event, and come back. Even though you have most of it covered with a good DJ, you always need to innovate with entertainment—new ideas, new themes, and new performers. For a few years, we were stuck with the same type of entertainment at every party, and we didn't realize how big the mistake was. People started to get tired of it; they started to try other parties with different ambiences and different people. The worst part was that we were not the only ones making the mistake, since a lot of the competition would copy what we did. So for a few years in Miami, there were a few simultaneous parties with a drummer and a couple of dancers. There were not many easy ways of getting out of that mistake, so in order to get those clients back on our side, we ended up having to do bigger events that people could not miss. We started doing live music events. Not the usual local bands that you could find every week, but internationally known artists willing to perform in nightclubs. There were fewer pros than cons in those, since it is very hard to make money in one of those concerts due to the cost of such artists. The good thing was that people did show up, and sometimes you would even make a little money after paying the artist. But in the long run, people started to expect more, our competition started to do the same, and it just became a game of the deepest pocket wins. This is not a good game to get caught playing when this is your main income. Unfortunately some people do this for fun and don't have the same needs that we serious people do.

I always recommend taking a step back and rethinking what you are doing. Look at what the competition is doing, but don't copy them ever. As a matter of fact, if they do something you were planning on doing, too bad. They beat you this time, so make sure you act faster next time. A lot of times you will find yourself hitting a roadblock. Your mind simply gives up on the creative process and shuts down without any new ideas. You might find yourself doing the same events over and over. Remember, just because these ideas worked once, does not mean they will be great every time. People want new places, new ideas, new parties. This is their time to unwind, and no matter how loyal they are to you, they will want to check out the new spot, new band, or new party that your competition started.

One thing I recommend is to take a vacation. In our line of business, taking a vacation is like going to work, but nothing will be more enjoyable. Even if you decide to take a vacation somewhere where there is no night-life, your brain will reward you as soon as you get back. Ideas will flow, and believe me when I say that you won't realize it, but wherever the vacation spot may be, it will always inspire the next party when you are a true nightlife entrepreneur. Let me give you an example. On our honeymoon, my wife and I decided to go to Bora Bora. There is definitely no prettier place in this world. Nothing could be more perfect when you want to relax and get your mind off any type of work. It is the closest thing I know to paradise. When we went there, we realized that there was nothing to do on the island. It was not a matter of not wanting to party; it simply was not an option. Not that I wanted to party, but we are always looking for the nearest bar just to see what they are doing different. Well, here there was nothing to do. For the first time in my life, I was going to bed an hour after dinner and waking up before sunrise. I did not see it at the time, but as we were living this experience, I was taking it all in and learning from it. One of the biggest lessons I learned from this trip was when we took a day off from hotel activities and spent it with a local. The island has about eight thousand locals, and they all know each other well. Their lifestyle is so simple. They eat the fish that they catch in the morning for dinner that night. If one has tomatoes and another has coconuts, they will trade without even considering the value of either one. These people are the happiest people I've seen in my life, and I come from a very happy place. But this was different. Our tour guide spoke to us about how the locals owned the land and rented it to the big hotel chains, and they had free education and hospitals. This was just too good to be true. Then he took us to his house for lunch. The house itself was something we consider more a shack than a house. It was all made of wood, and the windows were even open—no glass, no bricks, no big kitchen. It was very basic. But it lay about ten feet from the gorgeous sea. The wind was much cooler than any AC unit money could buy. The most impressive part was the view. Looking at the house alone, you would feel pity for this man and his family. But going in the house and looking out the window, I realized that he had the same view if not better than the one we were paying thousands of dollars a night to experience for one week. He had this for free every day of his life.

Anyway, I don't want to get all nostalgic and go into more detail about this man's happy life, but the bottom line is that I learned a great lesson that day. Life is about simple pleasures. And it was not until I got back that I realized that I needed to apply this to my life and to my work as well. Think of this. What would you rather have: a thirty-dollar martini in the lobby of a great New York hotel, made by the best bartender in the city, or a cold three-dollar Corona on a hammock in the Mexican Riviera over-looking the beach, with your significant other by your side? I don't have to think too much about this. From this moment on, I looked at the show very differently. Of course, there are all types of clients, cities, climates, and tastes, but in the end we all love life's simple pleasures. We went on to do our first cruise ship event to the Bahamas, and it was an unforget-table experience. Nothing fancy, just all you can eat, lots of beer, beautiful beaches, and friends and family.

There are other destinations where you vacation and go straight to the happening spots and start getting ideas. Las Vegas, in my opinion, is not a good option. It is a party town for sure, but I believe nightclubs in New York and Miami are much better. Las Vegas caters 100 percent to a tourist clientele, and when it comes to service, this is not always the best. I believe Vegas nightclubs are overpriced and just very predictable. Then there are places like Cancun, where you can find a gem like Cocobongos. I'm not even sure if this can be considered a nightclub; I mean, I guess you can be-cause of all the booze you will be consuming with their all-you-can-drink format. But this is more of a circus or theater than a nightclub. Don't get me wrong, I loved the place, and my wife and I had one of the best nights of our lives at this party. But it just does not work in a city like Miami where locals need to be included. You can't have a show that is the same night after night in a city where tourists like to go where the locals are. Then you have Bogota, Colombia, with its world-famous Andres Carne de Res. This place started as a barbecue on the side of the road, and I hear it now has over seven hundred staff members working a single shift. This is the kind of place you might not be able to copy just because of how expensive the labor alone would be in the United States, but you can definitely copy a lot of smaller ideas within this great spectacle as long as you don't look cheesy or like a bad imitation.

Another thing to keep in mind when talking about the show is women. Women are the most important part of the whole show. They are important in three ways. Number one, when it comes to picking the staff, make sure they are great looking. The more women the better, since most of the paying clients will be men. Second, you always want to have more girls than guys at your events. It just looks better. When it comes to girls, the more the merrier; when it comes to men, it is better to pick just the best ones. And last but not least, when you are planning your events, parties, decoration, marketing, and even the drink menu, you have to always keep the ladies in mind. Some of these things won't even be up to you at the beginning in this career, but there will come a time when your input will be not only accepted but also requested and needed. Never forget what women want. They will make you or break you.

I mentioned before that your staff needs to be good looking also. This does not mean that they only need to look good and not be good bartenders, for example. This simply means that the better they look, the better you will do in the end. Besides being good looking, there is something else that everyone can do, and that is look good. "Dress the part" is what we call it. This is a show and we all play a part in it, so if you want to be part of this select group, you'd better do your best to play the part. Personality is very important for both your staff and you. There are many things that are necessary if you want to do well in this business. Smiling is one of them. People don't like to hang out with someone who is always serious or grumpy. Believe me, I had a moment when I was getting tired of doing the same thing over and over, and I was forgetting to smile. As a matter of fact, I was not enjoying the moments I was sharing with these clients or friends. It had become just business, and this was a big mistake. We need to remember all the time that this is our clients' free time. We are here to make money, but they are here to have a good time. Think about those moments when you are out to dinner or at the movies. Imagine the server who is taking care of you at the restaurant with a face that says, "I want to go home." This will not make you feel welcome, and it will soon have you wishing to go home too. In our line of work, it is very important to be extroverted and outgoing. It is obvious that when it comes to promoting and building your clientele, you will need to be open to talking to different people all the time. There is very little room in this business for shy people. Besides extroversion being important when it comes to inviting new clients to your events, it is also necessary when it comes to catering to their needs during the show. It is not bad if people consider you courteous and charming as long as you control it and don't let it go to your head. I believe that if you have the talent to be humorous, that's a great personality trait to have and use with your patrons. People always like to hang out with those who make them smile. Just don't overdo it—you are not a clown.

Remember, this chapter is meant to help you understand the concept of the show from beginning to end. The show begins from the moment you decide to make this your business and your lifestyle; the show is not merely the night of the event. Whether there are bands, musicians, dancers, or performers of any type at the production during the night, they are simply a part of the show. Yes, they might be important at some point, and they might be even remembered by many, but don't forget that the most important part of the show is you yourself. Your staff will always try to reflect what you do. Dress the part and act the part, and those who follow you will do the same. Always set the right example. Smile as much as you can without looking crazy. Try to enjoy each moment you share with your clients as if they were your friends on a vacation in a faraway paradise. Forget that you are working, forget about the money, and make everyone—including yourself—believe that you are spending your free time at your workplace. Remember that if you love what you do, you will never work a day in your life. The idea is that you don't need to act the part

6

USE YOUR WEAPONS

If you happen to be a Republican who believes in the right to bear arms, I really hope you did not mistake my comment on using weapons as referring to those types of weapons. If that is the case, please put them away and get back to reading. (Just kidding!) The nightlife promotion is a very different game from most marketing, advertising, and promoting jobs out there. This is why it is so difficult for many people to make it in this business. Not having a book that tells us what to do, when to do it, and most of all how to do it makes our job a lot harder. We must rely on our creativity and, in your case, on books like this one from people who have already experienced the business firsthand. For the purpose of this chapter, we will call all the resources you use to bring people together at your events your weapons. These are as powerful as real weapons but without the damage.

Let's start with the common weapons that everyone knows or at least should know. The main one is advertising. This is usually very expensive and in most cases not used by a new promoter until he or she has reached a certain point in this career. There are many ways to run ads. Outlets like television, radio, magazines, and newspapers are all for some reason now called old school. They have always been expensive, but they used to be very effective. Designing print and video ads is a lot easier now because of the great supply of graphic designers in the market. You will find that graphic design has become one of the cheapest things nowadays. Even though there is a high demand, the supply is a lot higher, and with the growth of the Internet, you can now work with a graphic designer across the Atlantic Ocean and get the same work or even better for a fraction of the price. Just to compare, when I started my first parties, we had a friend who actually hand painted our flyers. We then made copies at a local Kinko's or copy store and delivered them, first by hand and then via mail to people's homes as our clientele database grew. This sounds like a million years ago, but it was only two decades, so it just goes to show that we must always stay on top of what is happening when it comes to technology and all these services. Very soon after our friend hand painted our flyers, we came upon a company that was innovating with graphic design and printing flyers. This was a big jump for us. It was not only cheaper, but also, instead of printing one thousand flyers, now we would get five thousand and in full color for the same price. Believe it or not, my father still keeps some copies of our first printed flyers. I never thought they would mean as much to me as they do—that and the fact that he kept them, I suppose. Back then everything came from our own creativity, so pretty much every weapon we used was not only new to us but also to everyone else.

Something else that we use today is called a street team. These are the people who distribute our printed material. Most people use six-by-four, printed, side-by-side, full-color, flyers. Our recommendation is to change that a bit so that yours stands out. Back then we had no street teams. We distributed all the flyers ourselves, going car by car outside of other nightclubs, inside parking lots, to the different colleges, and even door to door in some cases. Today we use different types of street teams. For example, my father is in charge of our day-to-day distribution during the daytime. At this time we send flyers and other promotional material to places like restaurants, clothing stores, and boutiques. Wherever you are posting flyers, it is a good idea to send someone who will be respected when he shows up to ask permission to place a flyer or poster. There is the regular street team that is used for events like concerts or sporting events. If you plan on promoting on all the cars, it does not matter who you use, but I recommend that you use a young and energetic group, at least two guys, to do this job. You never know who you might run into; some people just don't like flyers on their cars. Believe it or not, I was actually beat up many years ago just for passing out flyers to the wrong person. Nowadays we use a group of female models to promote at concerts. They pass out wristbands that actually get you in free at our after party. This works well if you are close to the place where the event is taking place. In this case we send four girls because it just attracts your attention more when you see four girls inviting you to an event. With concerts and wristbands, you want to get the people on the way out, so in some cases the girls will need to split, and it is better if they are never alone, so having four girls or more available is always better. Street teams are a must in areas with a high traffic of walk-by clientele. The team's job in that case is to wristband chosen people, and the way they get compensated is by a flat fee for the night, a per-hour rate, or simply a dollar amount per head. It all depends on your pockets and your needs. Street promoters often end up working for you as subpromoters, so it is important that you keep good track of the type of clients they are bringing to the table. Some main promoters or club owners pay a higher amount per head when the client is a girl than when it is a guy. This is again due to the effect of women on the whole show.

This brings me to your next weapon, maybe one of the most important if you wish to go from a promoter to a nightlife entrepreneur. This is your subpromoter. Subpromoters are all the promoters who bring you between ten and one hundred people. Don't think that it is easy to keep the good ones. Subpromoters who are able to bring one hundred people to your party will feel like they can do it on their own very soon, so it's in your hands to make sure they are happy working for you. Always make them feel like they work with you more than for you. In the end this is a business built on partnerships. Club owners need main promoters or promotional companies in order to make it unless they are a big brand with a big following, in which case they will still need promoters for the weeknights. So clubs partner with promoters to give them certain nights. On those nights you, the main promoter, will need to use subpromoters if you want to have a successful and recurring event. Subpromoters get paid depending on their productivity, and very few have salaries. I am not a friend of salaries in this business. Every time people have a salary, they feel they've already earned their money. The most common ending to relationships with salaried promoters is not a good one. People tend to get comfortable and not deliver when they're paid in advance or a fixed amount. There is no incentive to do a better job, and there is no loss if they don't deliver. I include myself in this equation. "No pain, no gain" is the saying. You want everyone involved to suffer if it doesn't work. This is the only way that everyone will be invested in the outcome.

A few chapters ago, we spoke about how important your database is. We said size matters. This is the time to use your most powerful weapon. Bring out the guest list, the client database—cell-phone numbers and e-mails. I recommend sending a weekly newsletter in which you include all your week's events and maybe your main event of the month. It is important to add content to these newsletters. People don't want to get a weekly e-mail just saying, "Come to my party and this is where I'll be." They want other information. Maybe add big concerts, your city's most important sport updates, the weather report for the weekend, some daytime activities, and coupons. You want people to actually open your e-mails and continue to allow you to reach them. Remember, they always have the option to opt out. If they do this, it means they are no longer interested. In that case you don't just lose a client, you lose information, valuable information that can be sold later to sponsors or others who want to use your database. The title in all these e-mails also needs to be catchy without being too obvious. You don't want to use words like "free" or "discount," because that will send most of your messages to the trashcan or junk mail folder.

You need to use your phone numbers the same way you use your e-mail data. At least once a week and even as often as once per event, you can call or text your clients. People have their phones on them at all times, so this is very direct. Even though this text blast will be massive because you can send it to your entire database with certain programs, you can make it very personal and direct to each client. Just remember that text messaging limits you to 140 characters in one message. Yes, you can send more than 140 characters and it will go through, but people will receive two messages instead of one, and believe me when I say they don't want that kind of spam on their phones. Think very carefully about who is on the other end of the phone before you write the messages. Separate your database, male from female. This might come in handy for many reasons when promoting and when using the data for other companies. Let's say that a certain new mascara came out, and the makeup company wants to use your data to offer the product to your clients. They might want all your data, but you can send one message to the women, offering the mascara, and a different message to the men, suggesting that they buy the mascara for the women in their lives.

When it comes to nightclubs, you could define your weapons as high range and low range. To understand this better, let's say that we can do mass promotion or direct promotion, meaning we either send information to a large number of people using one of the methods, or we use the method to send it to only one person at a time. There are some midrange weapons too, I guess, if you look at apps like WhatsApp. You are sending text messages directly to one person, but you can separate them in groups before you send the message, and this makes it massive. On the other hand, the person will get a direct message.

Let's compare the weapons and see how they work on the battlefield. We talked about flyers. There are different things you can do with a flyer. The first and most obvious one is leaving flyers in your own venue. These flyers will be left at tables or countertops at the bar. People will most likely not grab these flyers because they already are at your venue. But they will glimpse at them and learn about a different night or a certain special you offer during other hours. This is, in a way, a midrange weapon. It is not massive, and it is not one on one, so the possibilities of it doing the job are about fifty-fifty. Now let's say those flyers are handed out at a soccer game on a Wednesday night. You will most likely have two people handing out these flyers. They will each have about two thousand flyers. Let's say the stadium has about twenty thousand people inside. You send the people to separate doors and have them do all the cars. They each put flyers on one thousand cars, and then they head to the exits with one thousand flyers left each. They will give out one thousand flyers in about twenty minutes just to people rushing by them. Some people will get two or three flyers, and most people will read and throw it out in the next ten steps. Very few people will keep the flyer and read it later. Then people get to their cars, and two thousand of them find flyers there too. If you get lucky, those who received a flyer at the door will also have one on their car. This will stay with them the most. They will get that feeling that your event must be good if you are taking the time to give them two of these flyers. So during one event you've passed out four thousand flyers. Half of them were massive and the other half midrange, yet with some of them, you actually got the direct effect. In the end, about 10 percent of the people who got a flyer will actually consider going to your event, and about 3 percent will actually show up. But hey, 3 percent of four thousand is 120 people. Sure, you had to pay for the design, the printing, and the two people who gave them out. But I will spend $500 any day to get one hundred clients in the club. As a matter of fact, the average subpromoter in Miami gets paid five dollars per head in 2016. So clubs and main promoters are used to spending $500 for one hundred clients anyway.

Now I want you to compare another form of promotion, or another weapon that can be used from every range: your cell phone. I know that everybody seems to have his or her phone nearby all the time. In fact, it has become a problem for most relationships. The thing is that this problem has helped us reduce the gap between promoter and client. It can even be used to build clientele. It all depends on how you decide to use it. Let's start with what used to be the most common use of the phone, even though it is not what most people use the phone for anymore. As crazy as it sounds, it's the phone call. Oh God, that sounds so awful, so old school. I know you only use the phone part of your cell phone to call your mother because she is too slow texting you back and has not figured out a way to send you voice mail. Well, believe it or not, a phone call is the most direct weapon you have, and as much as people don't like to talk on the phone anymore, an unexpected phone call will go a long way. Nothing is more direct than a phone call unless you drive to each person's house and pay a visit, but I know you won't be doing that. You probably don't even know where most of these people live. How things have changed! Compared to all other weapons, the phone call provides the highest percentage of return on your investment. I know you need the phone anyway if you are a human. The time spent on a call does not need to be more than five minutes. This is because you will not make a phone call to say, "Come to my party on Friday." You will engage in an actual conversation, go back to basics for a few minutes. Enjoy the conversation. Ask how the person is doing, what he's up to, where she's been lately. Then go into what you are up to and say you hope to see him or her soon. This process has proven to be about 90 percent effective. Well, if that person don't show up that weekend, you'll see him or her the next. Do this with at least ten clients every day, and you'll see how you will never be hungry again. If you feel comfortable doing this with more than ten people a day, then by all means go ahead, but remember to keep up with everything you spoke about. You need to listen, be attentive, and actually care about these people who will be your patrons for life. Nobody else will call them, and in the end it is not about who has the best DJ or band. This is a business where the most important thing is feeling comfortable.

This brings me to the most important weapon that you will never use, yet it will be activated by your actions. You will not pull the trigger, but others will pull it for you. Imagine having a whole army working for you and for free. So what can be so good and you don't even have to do it? Well, it's called word of mouth. This is not earned very easily, because you need some time in the market to be even considered as a conversational topic, but the best way to earn your word-of-mouth rewards is with the personal touch. Make sure all your guests are having a good time and feel welcome. Make sure that you know them by name. Make sure to say hello every time, and don't do it from across the room. They want you to come over and ask them how they are doing. Do not hesitate for one second. You might even think you don't know them or that they don't remember who you are, but most likely they do. And if they don't, what is the worst that can happen? They will not make you look like an ass. In the end they are in your house. They want to hang with you and your girlfriends. They want to be part of your entourage. I am not trying to sound conceited; I just want you to be confident. You need people to be influenced by you.

People need a leader to tell them what is cool, what to drink, where to go, how to dress, how to dance or not dance. Most of the time they look to famous actors or singers when it comes to this. The funny thing is that we are the same as those big influences, just on a much smaller scale, yet we are closer to the people who look at us as influencers.

The idea of influencers is a new one that has come up within the past couple of years. The rise of the social media has built a new midrange weapon called influencers. So let's talk about influencers and social media. Neither was as important back when I started in this business, so I am definitely not an expert on the matter. But I do know that they are here to stay, and therefore, I need to keep updated in order to stay afloat when it comes to social media. Influencers are by definition people who affect the decisions of other individuals. The most common influencers have always been celebrities or athletes, like Michael Jordan and Tiger Woods influencing customers for Nike. The new trend changes the way this used to work for a reason that makes a lot of sense, especially with millennials making most purchasing decisions now. People don't trust an athlete who's paid to advertise more than they trust a midrange influencer giving heartfelt advice or comments on a specific product. Hopefully, the fact that these influencers are now getting paid does not mean it will affect the way they influence their followers. I believe that if they find a way to stay true to their beliefs, their influence will last a lifetime. On the other hand, if big companies win this war by making them influence people even though they don't believe in the product, people will see this and stop believing in the influencers. Influencers are not made through paid advertising. Those who want to follow them will. This is another reason why they are so powerful. People voluntarily watch their videos or follow their blogs and vlogs. It is not like being forced to watch a Budweiser commercial in the middle of the Super Bowl. It is very important for a promoter to study the influencers in their local area and figure out who caters to his or her needs, who has the right followers, what type of content they post, whether people engage with them, and so on.

After finding the right influencers, go old school on them. Try to locate them and invite them to your events. Let them have everything for free, and have them bring their friends. Just ask one favor in return for your hospitality. Ask them to post a positive review of their night. If you are in luck, you will be able to do so at no higher cost. Things are changing very fast in the social media world. First came Facebook, which my father uses daily, and then Instagram, where I post a daily photo of my family, my great diet, or the occasional party flyer. Now Snapchat has taken over. It's the quickest way to post, and that is what millennials love. (We'll see how Instagram does with their new Snapchat-like feature.) It is just very difficult for those of us in our forties to not look a bit ridiculous recording ourselves every five minutes in order to keep our history active and our followers growing. Whatever the next big thing is, just make sure you keep up, stay ahead. If a new app comes out, go for it. Try it, and don't worry about being different. This is a new era. Being different is the new normal. As a matter of fact, nothing is weirder than a regular kid who acts normal every day. With social media, remember to keep it about you and not about your business. Post some flyers once a week, but don't have an Instagram account filled with flyers and no photos of your real life. Blogs are getting more traction than old-style websites.

Even though any business needs to have a website, you could probably build a Word Press website and connect it to a blog where you post videos of things like your parties and your upcoming events. With promotion, there is not one thing that is bad to use. The more the merrier. Another reason to have a website is that you should post photos of your parties every night and update them weekly. You could either do this on your own or use existing websites that offer these services, like atnight.com. They will take the good-quality pictures, post them on their site, and even link them to yours. The good thing about those websites is that they also have traffic from other nightclubs, and that becomes a win-win for everyone.

If you are going to have your own website, the photographer is a very important person. Quality is a must. You want people to save these pictures and post them on their social media. These pictures should always be watermarked in order for them to promote your venue. It is probably also a good idea to come up with a hashtag to use for all the photos taken at your parties. This kind of keeps them all together in one big folder, and people get to see others who have also been there. This helps build your followers too. Websites have worked for the past fifteen years or so when it comes to building a database, especially because the photos are used to lure the clients into the website, where you can ask for their information in order to allow them to download their photos. The problem with this process is that people used to get home and go on their computers in order to do that. But things are changing very fast, and people want things like photos a lot faster. I have heard of a few people working on different apps that actually allow you to get the photos right away and still get users' data, which in the end is the most valuable asset. As a matter of fact, even my partner Gus is working on this idea, taking advantage of the fact that we understand our clients' needs. Who knows, maybe by the time the book comes out, this app will be out there, and it might even be our own creation. The point is that we need to stay on top of what is happening around us if we want to be a factor in this dog-eat-dog business.

Creativity is a must when it comes to promotion. This is something that you cannot learn; you either have it or you don't. Those of you who have it should make sure you take advantage of it. Never stop creating new ways to attract new customers. Always stay fresh with your events, promotions, specials, and even things as little as the text messages you send. Keep it fun and remember once again, if you love what you do, you will never work a day in your life.

Now let's have some fun. It's time for your first event.

7

IT'S SHOWTIME!

The moment you've been waiting for has finally arrived. You did all the hard work; now here comes the fun part. At least it will be the fun part if you make it so. This is that moment where you are working and getting paid to do this, but you should not ever feel like you are at work. This is one of the few jobs without a punch card, yet you'll still be on time. Don't forget that this is not someone else's party. This is always your party, your business. It doesn't matter what kind of deal you worked out with the venue; this night is your night. The more you look at it that way, the more successful you will be in the end. This is why I don't recommend doing this on a fixed salary. You will not be taken seriously when you have a salary, and you will not take it as seriously yourself. You want to be a part of this business from the get-go. It doesn't matter if you're working at a famous nightclub or an old bar in your neighborhood. If you love this job, you will make these nights great. Remember, in the end people are about having a simple good time. Don't try to overcomplicate things. Think simple. Good service, good product, good music, and good location will be the perfect recipe for success if they go hand in hand with all the promotional methods or weapons you've been reading about and all other weapons that emerge in this fast-moving market.

The night of your event is very important. On average you will spend six hours at each one of these, and if you are a hard-working promoter, that means you will have an average of three events a week. That is eighteen hours of your average forty-hour workweek spent only taking good care of your clients. This is why it is so important. Tip number one: do not skip this night. The minute that your clients don't see you there, they will find the next person to trust and to call for a reservation. Other promoters are always snooping around for this. As a matter of fact, not only do you not want to miss your events, but also you always want to be the first to arrive. This is the time when last-minute decisions are made, and you want to be a part of those. This is when furniture gets moved around, reservations are assigned, servers are assigned to sections, and the door sets up for the show to begin. In other words, though all these small details will not affect how many people show up this specific night, in the long run, it will mean a lot to your clients when they have a better table than others or get assigned the better server. The server will also remember the fact that you helped her take care of that big client. This is how you start building your clientele; this is how you earn their trust. Inviting them is very important; taking care of them is just as important. Taking care of a client does not mean necessarily letting them in for free at the door or getting them free drinks, although you will do a lot of that too. The idea is to make sure they feel at home and to do your best in making sure they have a good time. If you see that something is missing, this is the time you try and supply that to them.

Every venue will have a different rule when it comes to drink tickets and complimentary bottle service for promoters and their clients. It is good to have an idea of what you will need. This depends on how many subpromoters and performers you have working for you. At the beginning you might have to play it by ear. I have seen all types of systems for complimentary drink tickets. The most common one is getting a set number of drinks for your whole team. In my case we use four drink tickets per promoter. We give them two when they arrive and the other two when they reach a minimum number, ten being the most common. So if I have a team of twenty subpromoters, I will need eighty drink tickets in order to satisfy all my subpromoters' needs. I also ask for a bottle for any promoter who reaches over thirty people or sells at least four tables. This has become pretty much standard in today's nightlife in Miami. When we started doing this, there were no such things as drink tickets or bottle tickets. Back then there were so few promoters that it was a learning experience on the go, so it was more of an open-bar tab that was earned with trust. We started with getting drinks directly from club owners and managers, depending on how they felt about the sales. There was a club that gave us drinks based on the previous weeks' sales, and the complimentary drinks were not to exceed 10 percent of the total sales. What I am trying to say is that this is not written in stone. Most contracts won't even have this in them because it will be a different number every week. The bottom line is for you to realize that you are a partner in the night. You will most likely get paid a percentage of the sales. If this is not the case, you still are a partner because if it does not work for the owners, it will not continue. So the more free drinks, the fewer the sales. Of course, those drinks are a must in order to take care of good, loyal customers and promoters, but it is not a good idea to overdo this perk.

Some promoters are well known for taking extra care of their clients, with tables, complimentary champagne for all the ladies, no cover for anyone before midnight, extra drinks for promoters, and an over-the-top promoter table. They don't realize that in the end, they are slowly killing the business. Competition will end up having to do some of the same in order to not lose some clients, and the club owners will not be happy because of the direct effect on the sales and on the type of clientele that it will attract. After a while the club will start looking for new promoters to take over this night, and the only ones affected will be the promoters themselves, who will be out of a job. Luckily for us promoters, we can always look for a new venue. There is always a demand for our services due to the large number of clubs in a city like Miami. This might not be the case in smaller towns like Gainesville, for example.

The other thing that makes a great promoter is not jumping from one place to another. The real test is being able to stay on top at the same venue for many years. The two biggest ongoing parties that we have had as a company have been on a Thursday and a Saturday. Fridays are always harder, and we tend to jump around more on that night. This keeps our relationship with our customers fresh all the time, and it keeps us on top of the game as the number-one company for our niche.

A few moments ago I mentioned the promoter table. I'm not sure if you know what that means. Sometimes we have been in this business for so long that we believe everyone knows what we are talking about all the time. A promoter table is simple to explain. This is that one table in the nightclub where most people want to be. Why is this area of real estate so important and so tempting to most patrons? First of all, this is the table where the booze flows all night long. The promoter table used to be set up on the sides or in a hidden, unused corner with the sole purpose of serving drinks to the group of promoters and their friends. This idea has evolved over the years, and the promoter table has become more of a prime real estate idea. You will usually find a main promoter table in the middle of the action. This table is the one that will get the ball rolling for other big spenders in the club. Some clubs go as far as having different promoter tables in different areas of the club just to make the show a bigger one. The more realistic it looks, the better it is for the show and for the sales. Of course, all the liquor being poured at these tables starts as complimentary and for the sole purpose of taking care of subpromoters, main promoter, and mostly girls. The idea is to sell bottles to guys at this table too. This is that table where you will see a bunch of girls from the beginning of the night on. This is the table where everyone seems to be having a great time from the moment they arrive. Is it real? Well, it depends on who you ask. I am sure that if you have had the chance to spend a night at one of these tables, you might have a story to tell from that night. This is where most of the magic happens. If each table were considered an amusement park, this would be your Disney World. Make sure you understand that you are not a client. The purpose of this table is not to get you and your buddies drunk every night. The sole purpose of this table is getting the show started. Make sure you bring different clients over to your table every week. Let them experience what it is to party like a rock star without the large bill at the end of the night. But don't overdo it. If you see that the same client coming over to your table every week, give it a break. Make up an excuse. Say someone else is paying. In the end it is not all free. You need to pay the service charge, and on any given night, you are talking about $200 just in tips for four bottles. Imagine if you go all out. Tipping your servers and bartenders is a must, and it will pay off in the end. You need the staff to be happy and to take good care of you. A lot of servers don't want to take care of promoters because of the bad rep they have when it comes to tips. This is how servers make a living, so make sure they are well taken care of. They'll remember you when they have a big client and need a reservation at another one of your venues.

Now that I've mentioned not taking advantage of the promoter table just to get drunk, let me go a little bit deeper on that subject. Drinking on the job is not something you do in most jobs. Yes, this is a different type of job you've chosen, and having the occasional social drink will be almost demanded of you. But getting drunk is never the best idea. I'm sure things will get out of hands a few too many times, and you'll look back at when you read this for the first time and thought, "What is he talking about?" Then you'll understand what it is that I am talking about. There are many factors that will be affected by your drinking. Let's go over them quickly.

First, drinking affects respect from your peers and from your clients. This alone is more than enough reasons not to overdo it, but there are other things that will be affected, like being on top of your game. In my case there is something I cannot control: every time I have one too many drinks, I end up at the DJ booth asking for music that does not necessarily cater to the party but more to my own needs and wants. This happened so many times in the past that I once told DJ Willy to never listen to me again when I came up to him with any type of liquor on my breath. Not that he listened. I came up with a solution to this problem that worked for me: I don't drink between 10:00 p.m. and 2:00 a.m. By two I have done most of the important stuff. I've taken care of the music, the reservations, the clients, and the performers, and even closed the guest list at the door. I could even close the cover charge at that time and drink away. Not that this was the idea, but I could. What I actually do is have just a couple of drinks, with water after each one, which really helps. Remember that you will most likely be driving home. If you have had any drinks, get someone else to drive you, call Uber or a taxi, or simply walk home if it is close. Even better, eat after the party. There are always good stories to tell from the late-night dinner tables in the nightclub business. You also get all the inside info on how the other nightclubs did. Even though you shouldn't care, you will. Until you don't anymore. The only problem with the stories at these times is that half of them are made up. It's just the way this business rolls. It's a big make-believe world. Other promoters and staff members from different venues will be talking, and so will clients. Listen to the clients' stories more. They rarely have anything to gain from making up a good time. On the other hand, promoters and staff will know that the better they talk about their place, the better reaction they will have from possible new clients. The only times when you will hear a true recollection of the night's events is when it was actually great or when staff members are looking for a new job and can't keep from mentioning how slow their party was. Even though all of this is happening after the night is over, it is all part of the show, especially now that you have all these social media apps like Snapchat, where people are posting almost every minute of their lives, including when they come out of a nightclub. Fast-food photos and videos of their drunken friends are on the list of top posts for sure.

We've talked about the beginning and the end of the show, and we mentioned a few moments in between. Let's go over the middle of the show, the main event, the main act, whatever you want to call it. This covers everything from the moment the doors open to the public to the moment they close. This is on average six hours of operations from 11:00 p.m. to 5:00 a.m. Most clubs have three busy hours, like midnight to 3:00 a.m. And then there is the peak hour, usually 1:00 till 2:00 am. This will vary depending on the city you live in, the area your venue is in, the demographic you work with, and many other factors. The idea is to know what those hours are for your events. This will help you choose the perfect time for everything—performers, for example. Let's say you have a band playing. You need to make a decision: Do you want everyone to see this band, or would you rather they help you bring more people earlier? I've been on both sides of this decision. Our Saturday night party at Yage Bay Club that lasted over thirteen years was not famous for the artists that we brought to the club, though we did our fair share of concerts, even international bands. The purpose of having these bands was in part to bring a larger crowd to our weekly party, but mostly it was to build a name and create longevity for our brand and the nightclub. We would have the bands play around one thirty, the middle of the peak hour. These bands would play for at least an hour, which helped extend the peak hour on those nights, since the time the band was on was also a good time to go to the bar or order more bottles. On the other hand, we have had our Thursday night at Blue Martini for over nine years. Being that it is a weeknight and an older crowd, we have done the opposite when we bring a band to this venue. We promote the fact that the show will be at 8:00 p.m., so people show up earlier, yet we start the show at around nine and have it last no longer than forty-five minutes. What this does is bring a different crowd for the early part of this party that connects the happy-hour crowd with the late-night one. We call this transition, and it is just as important as the other two parts of the night because when you have a good transition, you are pretty much guaranteed a great late night. Of course, this works for this venue due to its location and demographic. Like I said before, this could change from place to place. The same place could even have different equations on different nights of the week. Saturday is always your biggest night; everyone goes out on Saturdays. Thursdays are your second-best night in Miami, because people are desperate to get out of the work mode. Friday is the third-best night overall, and some places work better on Friday than on Thursday, but this could be due to other factors like catering to a specific type of client who doesn't go out on Thursdays. Thursdays are well known for college nights. Fridays are for happy hours and for older crowds going out. Any other night of the week is just extra credit, so if you ever get one of those going, take good care of it. The longest-lasting parties are usually on days that nobody expects in cities like Miami where there are a lot of tourists at all times.

Now let's talk about live music. It is only recommended that you do big-name bands in nightclubs if you have a really good contact with their management, meaning you get them for a really, really good price. Most of the time, you will find that you work for them more than for yourself. I believe that when it comes to entertainment, you need to make a deal with the nightclub where they take care of this. This is one of the highest expenses, if you want to have events that people remember. Don't make the success of your night dependent on bringing hot bands to your club. People will stop going when there is nobody playing. It is better to build a nightclub based on other types of entertainment, good service, PR, and always a good local DJ. I was very lucky to have found a great DJ when I had just started in the business. Willy has been with us for over twenty years. I've had many other disc jockeys come and go, but he's become part of the family. As a matter of fact, the few times that we decided not to include him in the equation for various reasons, we ended up changing the plan and adding him later. He was the DJ for our two longest-running parties. In other words, he is the life of the party. The problem with many DJs today is that they want to become famous and produce their own music, mostly house music, which is not my niche. With Willy I never had to explain what I needed. He always knew how to handle the crowd.

If you are planning on doing this for a long time, and you want to do it on your own rather than for someone else, I recommend you build a relationship with an up-and-coming DJ who has the same vision as you. But make sure he knows what he is getting into. You are going to need his loyalty. This is something very hard to find nowadays. I am certain that our DJ has been offered more money many times before, but in the end he always stays true to us. If you trust your DJ completely like we do, you will not need to worry about the music. But if the DJ is not on the same page as you, then you need to stay on top of what the happening music is. Let the DJ know what type of music you want to hear at different times. Even more important, let him know what you don't ever want to hear at your parties. In my case we have a battle between the DJ and clients with a certain Latin style called bachata. I cannot stand most of it and neither can he. But a lot of clients ask for specific bachata songs, and they even go as far as offering to pay him just to hear a song. Most times the DJ wins the battle. Of course, everyone has a price (myself included, I just won't say what mine is).

So we went over the opening act, the final act, and the main act. Let's go back to the most important asset, your database. Remember how size matters? OK, this is that one time when your database will actually be called a guest list. You've done all your promotion, called everyone and his or her mother, texted, e-mailed, sent out flyers, and used all your social media. For the purpose of your night, your database will be shortened and called a guest list. Only two types of clients will appear on this list: those who asked to reserve tables and those you need to make sure don't get charged at the door. These include promoters, friends, family, and any important person you might know. There are different purposes for this guest list. The first one is assigning tables, which we did earlier. It is important to have your clients' cell-phone numbers on the guest list. This way your hostesses can call ahead of time to verify their time of arrival or cancellations. Another purpose is making sure that your real VIPs get treated accordingly. Make sure you always have this list separate, with no phone numbers in this case. You don't want to lose these clients to another promoter who gets his or her hands on the list, and even worse, you don't want the club owner to get a hold of it.

Then there is the subpromoters list. This list can be separated completely from the other two for two purposes. You need to keep track of which promoters showed up and when. A lot of companies track the comp tickets they give subpromoters on this same list. But the main purpose of the list is to keep track of how many people the subpromoters bring to the party. A separate hostess that most of the time works for the promoter instead of the venue will do this.

Next there is that list of everyone who said they were coming. Take a look at this list at the beginning of the night and go around the club looking for the people who said they'd come. It sounds crazy, but it works. Say hello to everyone you invited, write down who was there, and note who did not make it. This list will be important because it will serve as a guide to start your final part of the whole show, the follow-up. Following up is not only as important as inviting in the first place, but it is also the one thing that I can assure you most promoters only do with their closest friends. But how do you expect new clients to give you the same trust if they don't get the same treatment as your close friends? The list of people who didn't make it will be the first one you follow up on. These are the people you will call first the following week. Then you call the ones who went and got a table, ask how they were treated, and find out if there is anything you can do to make their experience better next time. Remember, all these phone calls start with a different subject other than your club. When you call the people who didn't show, for example, you might start with saying, "Hey, I didn't see you on Friday; is everything OK? You were about the only person not there. What did you do that night?" When you call the ones who did show, you need to thank them first and then go on to ask about their life. Finally you move on to calling those people whom you did not reach the previous week. This is how you not only build a larger database and clientele, but also you also earn their trust.

It's very important that you don't overpromise and always overdeliver. But if someone asks for something you can't give, say that you will do your best, and then offer something else instead of whatever he or she asked for. This is the little thing that will make his or her experience unforgettable. How many times has a nightclub called you just to ask how you are doing? Nine out of ten times, the answer is never. So be part of that 10 percent of promoters that consider themselves nightlife entrepreneurs. Build your client base, and remember the show is always on, so dress and act the part at all times. Now let's go to the next chapter to understand why you need to be everyone's best friend.

8

EVERYONE'S BEST FRIEND

Now that you have a better idea of what to expect when you throw your first party, event, gathering, or show, it is a perfect time to dig deeper into the type of personality traits you will need in order to have a longer career in this business. To be more specific, we will talk about your relationship with everyone who matters in this business, and that is simply everyone. So let's start to work on becoming everyone's best friend. Yes, when I say everyone, I mean everyone.

There are supposed to be five main core personality traits that divide into many other positive, negative, and neutral traits. The first thing we need to know is which of these traits define you. You may have an idea, but I do recommend taking a personality test, which will help you understand yourself better in the long run, and it will most definitely help you with any relationship. The five main core personality traits are said to be extraversion, agreeableness, conscientiousness, neuroticism, and openness. The good news is that I would consider only one of these traits to be a flaw when it comes to this business, and that would be neuroticism. People who tend to be neurotic may experience low tolerance to stress, emotional instability, irritability, sadness, and moodiness, among other negative traits. I don't think I need to get into why these traits could be a problem for the much-needed open, agreeable, and conscientious extrovert. People with an open personality tend to be very creative, curious, and imaginative. This will come in handy when you are in the creative process of the nightlife business. People who are well organized and very mindful of detail tend to be high in conscientiousness. As you could see in the previous chapter, there is a need for a lot of planning and organizing. Being trustworthy, kind, affectionate, and cooperative comes in handy when talking about your relationship with peers, and those people would be agreeable. The most obvious personality type that goes well with this business is definitely the extrovert. These are folks who are talkative, sociable, and have a higher than normal amount of emotional expressiveness. Now, if I were to describe a great promoter using only a list of personality traits, this would be the list: friendly, open, outgoing, well-bred, trusting, sympathetic, spontaneous, sociable, self-sufficient, secure, confident, responsible, popular, organized, modest, lovable, huggable, kind, leader, intelligent, creative, honest, honorable, humorous, hardworking, gallant, fun, focused, energetic, disciplined, courteous, charming, ambitious, and humble. Do you feel like I am describing you more and more? Or are you starting to run away from this career choice? Don't worry. These are all traits that would make the perfect promoter or nightlife entrepreneur, but we can't all be perfect. Just kidding. Yes, we can. Just kidding again. Or not. Oh well. Was conceited on that list? I don't think so. What I am trying to say is that we don't have to be all of those things, although the more the merrier.

Now that you know that you fit in perfectly and are ready to get the party started, let's look at how these personalities affect each relationship you will have during your life as a nightlife entrepreneur. Let's start with one that we have not looked at much in this book but that is very important in order to have a long-lasting party and career. This is your relationship with the club owner. Believe it or not, a lot of promoters never get to sit down with a club owner; sometimes they don't even know who the club owner is. My first recommendation is that if this is the case for you, stop whatever you are doing and request a meeting with the owner as soon as possible. It is very likely that at the beginning of your career, if you decide to become a nightlife entrepreneur instead of just a club promoter, you will work for smaller venues with lesser-known international names and DJs.

This doesn't mean that you can't make money as a promoter working for some of those big clubs. But the reality is that when you start your promoter life that way, it is very probable that you are cutting your promoter life-span a lot shorter. Not only that, but you are probably closing doors to become a nightlife entrepreneur later. The main reason this happens is because they will pay you well, give you access, give you drinks, let you share with their girls, and make you feel like family while you are promoting for them. But don't even think for a second about promoting for another club that might be their competition, and don't think that you'll get to sit down with the actual club owners. You'll have a weekly meeting with the management or sometimes even with a marketing director who will act like a club owner, and he or she will let you know how disposable you are and how unworthy of being there. This is why I always recommend going the other route and working for yourself or a big promotion company that you can partner with later.

Now that I got that out of the way, let's go back to those who've decided to start their own business or to work with a big company and start at the bottom and work their way up. Those promoters will actually get the chance to meet the owners of the clubs, bars, or restaurants where they will be hosting their weekly events. It is very important that you start on the right foot from the beginning. The first impression is the one that matters most. The good thing is that you get two chances of a first impression if you do this first meeting right: the actual first impression when you get your deal, and the second first impression after your first performance. Both of them are equally important, even though it is likely that if you don't leave that first meeting on a good note, it is very likely you won't make it to the big show.

The nightclub promoter name has earned a bad reputation with a lot of club owners over the past few years. One of the main reasons this happens is because of the lack of regulation and education. This does not mean that a promoter will not be well educated or will not want to do things right, but there is not one promoter that can start this business knowing what to do, simply because there is no school for it. Yet. You need to keep in mind that club owners will go to a meeting with a promoter not because they want to but because they see us as a necessary evil. This is not only due to the bad reputation promoters have gained over the years, which we will fix together, but also because meeting with a promoter means two things. First, it means that the club owner could not do promotion successfully on his or her own. And second, it means that the owner needs your help to build the business. Nobody wants to admit that he or she needs someone else to bring in business, especially someone who's young and has no education in the field. This is why it is so important for you to go to this meeting well dressed and well prepared, as you will be thanks to reading this book. After you have had a few jobs and managed a few nights in different clubs, you will know exactly what a club owner wants to hear at that first meeting. But this is your first time doing it, ever. Where do you get the information you need in order to convince an owner to give you the job over all other promoters and companies out there? What is going to be the difference between you and the marketing firm he paid thousands of dollars and that never delivered? This will be different in every case, which is why I say that you need to come prepared. Research is always important before a big meeting. The owners want to hear you say the right words, and they want to believe you can fix their problem. If they didn't, they wouldn't even consider meeting with you. The bottom line is making them feel comfortable. Make them understand and believe that you are there to make their business profitable and better. You are not there to take a chunk of their existing business; you are there to bring them new business and to build a long-lasting relationship. The average life-span of a party in a city like Miami is less than a year. This is very short term. It makes no sense whatsoever for club owners to give up a percentage of their sales for a short period of time and then lose the party to the club next door. They need to feel that they can trust you. There need to be contracts—not verbal but in writing. A contract with a trial period of three months and then the option to renew for a yearly contract may be the way to go. This makes you look more professional than half the promoters out there, who run this business the same way they would a lemonade stand on their front yard.

You also need to study very well what profit margin this type of businesses has. You want to ask high in order to give yourself some negotiating room. Every club owner wants to feel he got a good deal by lowering whatever it was you asked for. But at the same time, you can't ask so high that an owner won't even counter or that it might affect his overall business. The only way a nightclub-and-promoter deal works is if you think of it as a real partnership. They have the venue, they have the staff, and they have the product, but you have the clientele; you have the capacity to make their business profitable. More than that, you need to see the venture as your own from the minute you strike a deal. It can't be looked at as two teams. You need to be on the same page. If you make money, they need to make money, and vice versa. There are many types of deals and different possibilities. Every case will be completely different from the other, and there are many factors to take into consideration when entering into a partnership or joint venture like this one: How many partners will there be? What night of the week will the event take place? Did the nightclub have any sales before? How many promoters will you have working with you? Do you want to make a percentage of sales? Do you want a salary? What guarantees that you give to and get from the owner? Do you pay for your drinks, or do you get complimentary tables? How often do you get paid and on what day of the week? Who pays for entertainment? Door staff? Can you bring your own people to work for the event? Do you keep the whole door, or do you split it? I could go on and on talking about the different deals, contracts, agreements, and clauses, and I would never be done. There is only one way that we can make this easy, and that is by regulating the system. But for now, it is really all up to your basic negotiating skills.

So step one is to make sure to have a great first meeting. Work on the relationship with the owner. Make him or her trust you. Don't overpromise, but make sure to let him or her know that if you get everything you ask for, you will have a successful, long-lasting business together. The second nightclub that I ever worked with, Southfork, started with a one-hour conversation with the owner inside the business, not even talking about us promoting it, just talking about the potential the place had. This venue could fit about a thousand people, but it only hosted about fifty patrons on a regular basis. The owner, Dennis, was a good businessman, but more than that, he was a great man. After an hour talking about the reasons why he thought his business was not doing better, we said we had an idea to propose to him. We simply believed so much in this venue and the man behind it that we made him an offer he could not refuse. We offered him a first party where he could see the type of people we could bring to his venue, and we did not want any agreement. We said simply that we would trust his judgment after the event took place. To make a long story short, that party lasted fourteen years, and it even included an additional construction a year later so we could host eighteen hundred people instead of a thousand. We did not have the best deal we've ever had for our side at this venue, but we did have a long-lasting, productive venture that brought profits to both sides. And even more important, Dennis became a friend and our first mentor. So if you feel confident enough about what you can bring to the table, don't be afraid to trust the other side and show what you are worth. You might even get a better deal after you've shown your part of the deal. Now, if you don't feel that confident, then there might be something you are not doing. Maybe it's not the right place or the right time. It is very important that you do not start a new venture just because you need the money. Make sure it is the right place, the right time, and the right owner willing to give you the right deal first.

After you have developed a good relationship with the club owner and have struck a deal, the next person you need to build a relationship with is the general manager. Most nightclubs have a GM that will meet with you on a weekly basis and that will be the go-to person for most of your issues and concerns. This will also be the person who will work with you on making everything happen. Even though the owner will give him or her directions, he or she is the one with the experience and the ability to make your life either miserable or plenty of fun. Make sure to take this person's phone number right away. The first advice I can give you regarding the GM is to never go over him or her and talk to the owner about something you could resolve directly. This is a rule that could make you or break you in this business. Managers will move around from one club to another. They will always have a way to pull strings; they can get you those extra drinks and a better table if you just stay on their good side. As a matter of fact, I will give you an extra tip that will work wonders. Write down the manager's birthday. Don't miss it, and always give a gift. Believe me when I say you will be the only one doing so. These people are the closest there is to you in the club. Remember, you don't work for the club; if you've struck the right deal, you have a partnership with it. So the GM is the person who can make your new business a success if you do your part by bringing your clients, and he or she can use things like good service and great drinks to make sure those clients come back. If you see a possibility to develop an actual true friendship with the GM, I would highly recommend it. You will probably have a lot in common anyway. I am very glad to call Berto, the managing partner at Blue Martini, a great friend and also a mentor like Dennis, the Southfork owner. It is not a coincidence that these are our two longest-lasting parties.

Forming relationships with the staff in general is very tricky, because you will be working with many different types of people. But usually, if they are in this business, they are likely to be outgoing and willing to meet new friends. Just like promoters, bartenders, servers, hostesses, barbacks, and bussers need to be people persons. Their number-one job is service. Their hours will be even worse than yours, so you will be spending a lot of your time with them. Think of them as your new extended family. These are not your employees, even though this might be your business, and in some cases they will be doing what you ask. It is very important to remember that they work for the club, which means they only work for one person, and that is the GM, not even the club owner, unless you are working for a very small nightclub or neighborhood bar. This is probably the only case where you will see the owners giving direct orders to staff members. Nightclub staff members have an even shorter life-span than that of promoters due to the high demand for being fit, good looking, and outgoing. Clubs are always on the lookout for newer, better, faster, better-looking, and, yes, younger bartenders or servers. This means is that you will see a lot of them come and go, but it does not mean that you don't need to be their friend or rely on them to better serve your customers. It actually means you need to always be open to meeting new servers and to give them the same respect you have been giving the older ones who have been with you for years.

Another good reason to make sure you keep a close friendship with all staff members is the fact that you never know when you might need their recommendation at a new club where they are now working. As a matter of fact, my second-largest party, our Thursday night at Blue Martini, has been going on for over nine years. A bartender who was dating one of the owner's sons brought me in. She had a lot of pull when it came to him making a decision, and she had worked with us at our biggest club for a few years before that. She knew the numbers we could pull, and she also knew the clientele, so it was a win-win situation. Ten years later, she is retired, happily married, and one of our good customers now. We are still there, and everyone is still very happy with that venture.

The last thing I am going to tell you for now about the relationship with your staff coworkers is probably the most important and the most overlooked by any promoter out there. This has been something that has set us apart from others and has helped us with our promoter–staff member relationship. It has even helped with the managers' and owners' relationships, because they want nothing more than to see their staff happy. This valuable tip is going to sound simple, but for some reason not everyone understands it as such: tip your servers and bartenders. Yes, as simple as that may sound, it does wonders for your business. We even include it as a company expense. Some nights we might not even get as many drinks or bottles, but we know that these people work hard for their money and that they are still only getting paid minimum wage, so if they don't get good tips, you will lose them. Also, you don't want to hear a group of servers complaining because they don't want to take care of the promoter's table. That is just sad. Nothing makes me happier than to know that all the staff we have been working with over the years have been well taken care of.

The only people in this business who will always be working for you directly are your subpromoters. It really all depends on the type of promoters you have on your team. From experience I can tell you that the hardest thing to find is a subpromoter who does the job exactly the way you want him to. And when you find one of those, he'll believe he wants your job the first time you let him know he did well. Before you know it, he is your new competition. This makes the promoter-to-promoter relationship one of the most complicated ones in the business.

Let's start with the first type, the main promoter and subpromoter relationship. When you are a main promoter at a nightclub, as I said before, you are a partner in this specific night. This is your business. You will be the one with the responsibility, the one doing all the work that nobody sees during the week—putting together upcoming events; dealing with the DJs, entertainment, and staff; meeting with the GM; talking occasionally with the owners. The subpromoter has one job only, and this is to bring people to the party on that specific night and be there to make sure they are taken care of. Depending on your deal, either the main promoter or the club will pay the subpromoters. Subpromoters work directly for the main promoter and have a weekly meeting at the venue with the main promoter and all other subpromoters to discuss the good and the bad and to get paid. It is very hard to have a good relationship with a good subpromoter, because all she will see in the end is how many people she brought to the table. Therefore, when she is good at that, almost every time she will believe she wants to take over. Subpromoters also often want to go directly to the club owners or the GM. This is not acceptable, but there is nothing you can do about it unless you have a good written contract that protects you from any of them leaving and taking other subpromoters with them. The point I am trying to make is very simple. There is nothing legal you can do in order to stop this. The only thing that will help you avoid this problem with promoters and subpromoters is to follow three basic rules. First of all, work hard every week to make sure that you are still the top producer. This is a business where you are only as good as your last party, and one bad week can make some people lose respect for you. Second, make sure to have a good relationship with every one of your subs. Don't ever talk down to them, let them speak up, and make sure that if they bring something to the table, you will consider it, and if it is a good idea, you will also make it happen. Let them know that you are proud of the work they do, invite them you your own table every once in a while, give them a call during the week, worry about how they are, and get to know their families. Know them better than you know yourself, if possible. They will be your most powerful weapons and the most lasting relationships you will have in this business—that is, if they are any good. Believe me when I say that. This even goes for those that leave. This brings me to the third rule, which is simply to have a good contract and a good lawyer. This has been my biggest flaw throughout my career. It would have helped if I had taken a class on nightlife law, or if there were any law, for that matter. It sounds conceited when I say that everyone I've considered my competition throughout the years has at some point worked for me or with me, but it is completely true. I have always believed that competition is healthy, but it tastes a lot better when you are on top. The relationship between you as a main promoter or company and other promoters or promotion companies gets a lot more complicated when they have worked for you and decided to do their own thing, but it is almost impossible to stop this from happening. Everyone deserves a chance to do his or her own thing anyway, and believe me, if it's the case that your best promoter leaves you to start a new company and becomes your competition, it is kind of like watching a son grow up. It just gets complicated when you remember he knows all your secrets, all your tricks, and sometimes all your good clients, so it is actually better if you help him grow with you.

The best-case scenario between you and a great subpromoter is actually what I wish would be the story of you and me. I want you to become a great promoter. I want you to start working with my company. I want you to become my junior partner. In the end we can partner up and take advantage of my experience and of your youth and will. At the same time, I wish for you to do things better than I ever did. So with that said, let me tell you where I believe I went wrong in my relationship with other subpromoters and other main promoters. The first mistake was not having some kind of written agreement. This should be a must in this business, since you will be sharing a lot of information with them. You want to be on the same team for as long as possible. When it comes to a promotional team, yes, you want to have the best promoters in the city, but handling a group of the best is not an easy task, so the more the merrier. It doesn't matter how bad some of them might be at this job. As long as they bring new clients to the table and follow your advice, keep them around. You never know when a slow season might hit you. Then treat them all the same when it comes to respect and the way you give orders, but of course, make sure the best ones always get a taste of the perks that they have earned with hard work.

Probably the number-one rule to keeping your team together, and growing it, for that matter, is making your weekly payments on time. Since our early days, we've scheduled our weekly meetings on Tuesday, and it has stayed that way. There have been only a few times when we found ourselves in a position where we couldn't pay promoters on time. This is not a good idea. They are promoters for a reason. They know a lot of people, and they get the word out. Imagine what a group of, say, thirty promoters who haven't gotten paid can do with their mouths in one week. You also have to put yourself in their shoes. A lot of them need this paycheck to get by on this week's payments, and more than that, they did their job. So pay on time.

Then there is that other matter of trust. Hey, I am all for it. But don't. I've seen it all: The obvious promoter that you always knew was going to leave you. The best friend who stabs you in the back. Your best promoter who gets a better offer at another venue or company. And worst of them all, the right hand who decides to form his own company from within your own and offers your whole team a new alternative with better pay and more perks. Whoever it is, just be sure to know who you can trust, and when you do, don't give them everything. I once started to build a great teacher-pupil relationship, one that went on for at least five years. I felt I had found the person who was going to continue our legacy without changing our values and who had the same basic morals. Yet when given the chance, he didn't think twice about starting a new company using a lot of what we had taught him and taking a few of our team members. The battle between his company and mine has been ongoing for almost a decade already. A lot of promoters and venues have worked for both of us. For some very strange reason, people seem to like the Coca-Cola-versus-Pepsi type of wars. Like I said before, competition is great, as long as it is healthy and has its boundaries. The problem is that since this business is not regulated much, people can do what they feel like without any code of honor or respect for hierarchy. Therefore, don't build a workforce, build a family. And once more, remember that you need to be everyone's best friend, from the club owner to the GM to the staff and the subpromoters. But keep your inner circle close and your possible competition even closer. Just don't give everyone access to all your weapons. You never know when they might be used against you.

9

LOCAL CELEBRITIES

We've come a long way since you picked up this book. We spoke about how this is not a hobby for you and how you want to build a career. Then we talked about the type of promoter or nightlife entrepreneur you wanted to be. Then we focused on the importance of controlling your money and costs. In the next chapter, we discussed the importance of your database or guest list—remember "size matters"? The next topic was all about the show, followed by the use of your arsenal of weapons in order to pack your events and then actually run the night from beginning to end. And just now we went over the importance of your relationship with pretty much everyone you will be working with. At this point you should have a strong idea of what it is to be a nightclub promoter, subpromoter, or even a main promoter at any venue. In this chapter I want to talk about a subject that might be left behind in most cases because others might not see its importance but that I believe is part of your total package and will help you have a longer-lasting career.

When you read the words "local celebrities," what is the first thing that comes to mind? Do you think of rock stars? Red carpets? Do you see others as the celebrities, or do you see yourself as the celebrity? These are all important questions you should ask yourself in order to understand how you feel about your new job, career, or lifestyle. There is really no right answer to these questions; they simply tell you a bit more about where you are today and where you might want to be.

It is very common for most people to want to live the lifestyle of the rich and famous. That is until they actually get the chance and realize it's not that much fun all the time. There are so many things you give up as a celebrity. Of course, I am talking about people like rock stars, athletes, and actors. If you've ever run into one of them at a restaurant, club, or on the street, you know what I'm talking about. They may always get special treatment, but there are very few places that they can actually enjoy without being bothered. And this is a problem that increases in direct proportion with their success. The bigger the celebrity, the harder it is for them to hide. Of course, being a celebrity has a lot of perks and advantages, starting with big paychecks and including things like mansions, trips all over the world, and private planes. But what about the most precious gift of all—privacy? What about being able to do what they want, when they want, and where they want? Sometimes all the money in the world is not enough to buy those few moments with your newborn and wife on a regular public beach. Sure, flying to the Maldives with them is great, but what if all you have is a couple of hours? Celebrities have to work a lot of hours to get to be that famous. If you ask me, there is no way I would trade my place with theirs at any moment, just for that reason alone. I love my privacy, my space. My time. I'm not sure how you feel about it, but I believe I have good news for both of us. I was talking about big celebrities, and this chapter is more about someone else: local celebrities.

What or who is a local celebrity? Well, the name itself explains it. It's anyone who is treated as a celebrity in your local area. Let me use an example. The mayor of your city is not very well known in other countries; as a matter of fact, he or she might not even be known in other cities within the same state or county. I am from Miami, and the mayor of Miami is without a doubt a local celebrity in my city. Miami is filled with local celebrities; there are always many TV personalities roaming around the nightlife scene in Miami. This might sound corny, but in my niche, I handle a lot of local celebrities from the soap opera world. You might have no idea who they are, but they are on national television day in and day out.

It is very important to understand the difference between an international celebrity and a local celebrity and most of all to know how to treat each of them. The hardest job is keeping up to date on who is a local celebrity. The crazy thing with local celebrities is that they might be up there today and nowhere to be found tomorrow, but I believe that if they've been up there, they have earned their spot. Not caring about a local celebrity because his or her soap opera character died in an accident is like not taking care of Pete Sampras because he is not as good as Rafa Nadal today. Or like not caring that Lebron James walks into your party because he is no longer with the Miami Heat. Some people simply earn their status and should always be taken care of the same way. A lot of times in the nightlife industry, you might find that your best celebrities are the has-beens, as some call them. I prefer to say that if they have been, they will always be. So take good care of these people.

The treatment you give a local celebrity might be different from that of a big celebrity. The first thing is that big celebrities are not really looking for free stuff. The most valuable gift you can give them, as we said before, is their privacy, their space. The easiest way to make sure that a big celebrity becomes your best client is by making sure of two things: that there are no photos, and that the celebrity trusts you. When I say no photos, I mean just that. No pictures with staff members, no pictures with promoters, and no pictures with patrons. This is very hard to do, but you can do your best to make this happen. A lot of times celebrities will even say it's OK. Well, it's not. They are on their night out, enjoying their friends, and the last thing they want is to be taking photos with people they don't know. They will do it because they are people persons, as are we, but it's not what they want. Our job in this case is to understand their needs and meet them in the best way possible. If you have a security guard available to help with this endeavor, it is even better. The owner of the club will usually let you know if it's OK to take a picture of celebrities at the end of the night or right before they leave. But I recommend that you don't use any pictures for promotional material later. Instead, get the word out right away. Let people see them, ask them to tell others, and have your staff get the word out the same night. Everyone will start talking about the celebrity who went to *this* club. Guess who will be the first ones to find out? Other lo-cal celebrities. If an international celebrity visits one venue in your city, I promise you that all the local celebrities will be lining up the following weekend not only to see what the hype is all about, but also to be seen at the new happening spot that they don't know they are helping become the hip place. Make sure that you are always informed about who is in town when it comes to big celebrities. It might be even good business to book one of them as a guest host if it is something your people enjoy. There are some demographics that could actually not care less if they are sitting next to Madonna; all they want is good service. But most often everyone would love to party with the stars, and the bigger the star the better.

The second thing that international celebrities and local celebrities both need is to trust you. They want to have a promoter on speed dial so that every time they go out, they can get the star treatment. But more than that, they want to know that if they need to not be seen that night, they won't be seen. This is very big with athletes. I've taken care of MLB players who have been at the club till 5:00 a.m., gone out with our staff to an after party till noon, and then gone on to pitch the worst game of their lives the next day. If we were to let this kind of information out, it could cost them their jobs. Lucky for them, we learned fast that it was better to keep this kind of information secret instead of divulging it and using their names to promote our parties. And lucky for us, they realized they could trust us, and they became our loyal customers very quickly. At the very beginning of our promoter life, we had a great visit from the New York Yankees, who were in town to play the then Florida Marlins. One of my good friends, who managed a salsa singer, was contacted by one of the players who knew the singer. The player wanted to know if my friend could recommend a good place to go out where the players would not be seen much. I didn't even know they were coming till they showed up. It was almost the whole team. This was when the Yanks were killing it, so anyone who knew anything about the sport knew who they were. It was impossible to control, and in a matter of minutes, we had to take them into a smaller room that was not even open that night. It probably wasn't the best experience for the players, but it was great publicity for us—the following week we could not handle the crowds who were showing up to see who might be around. It definitely helped us, even though if this were to happen today, they would have killed me because they would have been all over social media in a second. For sure, though, that club was a success with local celebrities for months to come.

It is very important to know when it is good to promote a celebrity's presence at the club and when to keep it quiet. You will always communicate the fact that he or she was there; you just need to know how and when to do so. Cases will vary, and you will see all types of attitudes about it. It really depends on the celebrity's personality and how famous he or she really is. From my experience, I would sum it up like this. The most famous celebrities don't want to be bothered; the fewer people they have to see on their way in and out the better. They are still there to have a good time, but they just need to feel like regular people once in a while so they don't go nuts. Then there are the normal, average celebrities who like their space but don't mind taking the occasional photo just to keep them out there on other people's social media. For some strange reason, people who meet celebrities and take a picture with them feel a special bond with those celebrities afterward. People seem to feel as if they actually know the celebrity. This is weird but real, and I see it a lot. Then there are the local celebrities. Most of them like to be seen and talked about, so they want the best table you can give them in the middle of the club. They want to come in at the peak hour so that everyone is already there and nobody misses their entrance.

Finally there are the struggling celebrities. I'm not sure if they belong in a whole separate category or if they don't belong on the celebrity spectrum in the first place. In any case, these are the has-beens, those that need and miss the limelight. Some even have to manufacture publicity. I've seen things as crazy as a reality TV show that told everyone that their star was the owner of the nightclub where I was promoting, and I knew that this was 100 percent false. The star would just show up one day of the week and film as if he were going to meetings, and then they would film on a weeknight to make it look like it was the actual nightclub during the weekend. This really bothered me because I believed in reality TV before that. No more Kardashians for me. Once we were paid to let some photographers in the club to take some photos of a famous couple. When they arrived, I realized that the celebrities were not even a couple. They were simply making people believe that they were together because they needed to be on the news. The photos that ran on every Spanish network TV show made it look as if the paparazzi had caught them by surprise. What bothered me the most was that the photo credits and the newscasters were identifying the club as one in a whole different city, so we never even got credit for it. I can only imagine the load of crap that we are fed every week in this showbiz world.

Well, in the end it doesn't matter. What does matter to you and me is understanding what role these local celebrities play in our own show. We need to know what to do with each and every one of them—how to treat them, when to bother them, when to stay away, when to take special care of them, and when to let them be. There are three artists who have been very important for me for different reasons. Some of their stories have stuck with me the longest because they were not only great for my niche, but they are from my country of origin, Colombia, and from my local area, Costeños. These three celebrities are Carlos Vives, Sofia Vergara, and Shakira. Unfortunately for me, two of the three stories did not end well for my company or for me personally, but at least my conscience is clean.

First there is Carlos Vives, one of the biggest singers from my country. Due to being at the right place at the right time, I had the opportunity to produce and promote three small concerts with him on three consecutive Thursday nights at a local small venue next to the Miami River a few years back. This was an amazing experience because Vives wanted to rebuild his relationship with a specific demographic, and at the same time, he was considering buying this venue to open a new business with live music. I was lucky to have been in charge of making this happen and am very proud to say that even though the one clause we had in our verbal agreement was to not promote to the masses, we were still able to pack it all three weeks. Everything was great, and Vives was loved by everyone. He did something not many artists do: he went from table to table, singing and asking people what songs they wanted to hear. People did not believe this was happening. This was an artist who packed American Airlines Arena in Miami. How could this be possible? Well, everything was great until the third week, when Vives arrived and saw signs from radio stations, liquor sponsors, and a line that went around the corner outside of the venue. The minute he saw this, he was simply mad or disappointed, for lack of a better word. He was well within his rights to be upset. We had agreed that this was not going to happen, but the owner of the venue figured that it was better for his business to forget about this agreement and bring as many people as possible to this last event. The problem was that my company's name was the one caught in the middle between the venue and Vives, so needless to say, this was the last chance we had to do something with one of our idols.

Then there was the time that Sofia Vergara came to my birthday celebration. This was already a great gift, but it got better as the night went on. She is probably one of the funniest people you could meet. I was and still am very good friends with her sister Veronica, who brought her that night. As soon as she came in, we took her into the main VIP area, where she was out of the reach of most people, especially paparazzi. To make a long story short, we all had a great time that night, but little did I know that there were freelance paparazzi inside the club. Even worse, one was inside the VIP. It was probably less than a week later when I found myself on the cover of a national magazine with Sofia Vergara. This would have been great if many things had been different. First, I wish we had known they were taking pictures. This was probably the worst photo they ever posted of her. The caption next to the photo said "*pasadita de felicidad*," meaning that she was extra happy, but due to the way it looked, there were two stories they were trying to sell. The first was that she was on something. Believe me, she was not, and she does not need to be. The second story was that we were some type of couple. The worst of this is that we both had partners at the time, so it didn't go well for either of us. I'm not sure what I could have done to prevent this from happening, but I do know that it ruined a relationship with someone who could have been my best celebrity friend. I was never even able to fix this because the magazine went on with the story for a second edition. It's crazy to read the things they write, knowing they are not true. I can't imagine how much of what they post online today is false. I also wonder how many serious relationships this has harmed or ruined.

Then there is the time when Shakira came to one of our Carnaval de Barranquilla events, where three thousand people danced and covered themselves in flour. There was no way that she could show up at this event and not be run over by the crowds, especially because she is so petite. The good thing is that she came up with the idea of wearing a traditional monocuco costume that covered her face. She was actually barefoot and jumping up and down among her biggest fans without anyone knowing she was there. Did she ever come back? No. But she made my day.

So it doesn't always go the way you want with celebrities, but you need to try to do your best or someone else will, and that person might be the one to take away from your business. One way to make sure that you at least look like you care is by comping local celebrities every time they come to the club. Don't let them wait a minute at the rope; get them VIP access right away, and have a table ready for them at all times. I mentioned before that big celebrities are not in it to save money when they go out, but local celebrities are not as wealthy as you might believe, and the best investment the club can make is to give them free food or liquor. The minute they arrive, make sure that you are the one to go take care of them. Club owners are not always interested in a relationship with the local celebrities; they feel that all the celebrities do is come and drink their inventory. Remember that you are the expert on the subject, and that the thirty dollars a bottle might cost you will go a long way. It is also very probable that a local celebrity has a local entourage, and there is nothing more important than creating a local client base. You can't build your business on tourism, even though some clubs that do well in the city cater to a high percentage of tourists. But this is not the promoter's main job. Although some promoters may consider tourism as one of your thousand weapons, the best way to go about reaching tourists is through hotel concierges. This is an easy task. Simply create a system that pays concierges like subpromoters for all the people they send you. Attack the hotels near your venue first and go from there.

Another thing that might come as a surprise is that concierges might know what celebrities are in town, and they get direct access to them. People at five-star hotels see a concierge as the guy with the crystal ball that has all the answers and the best recommendations to the most happening spots. See concierges as extended promoters. Treat them just as well, and make sure they get everything they are ever promised. Some want money, others want perks. They have a way of turning perks for hotel guests into money for themselves.

Use the old-school power of the trade when dealing with people like concierges. Before there was any currency going around, people traded goods or services without the use of money. It was called bartering. Not too common nowadays. Let's see it in a quick mathematical equation. Say a hotel guest goes to a nightclub and buys a bottle of Grey Goose vodka. Today that would cost between $250 and $400 in Miami. If you as a promoter give that same bottle to the client through the concierge, it will cost the club owner about fifty dollars, tax included. And it would cost you about the same in the commission that you won't receive. But it ends up being a win-win situation. The concierge takes care of the client by getting him or her a complimentary bottle, but this has a small clause with it: sell them at least one more. The hotel guest also wins because, well, they get one free bottle, and even though they will have to tip for it, they've still saved at least $200. The server wins because he or she still gets tips and a good new customer. The club owner wins because giving away a fifty-dollar bottle will generate sales of at least one additional bottle, usually more. Last but not least, you build clientele and sales. Of course, this can't be done with every client, but the purpose of talking to the concierges is to learn who is in town to spend money versus who is just going to take advantage of your generosity. Remember, nothing is free in this world. It is the same in this business. You will see a lot of complimentary drinks and tables going to VIP clients and celebrities, but in the end they are always attached to a sale. The job is done well when only you, the owner, and the manager know about the whole equation. The customer simply feels special. How many times have you heard the words, "I'll give you this discount this time because it's you, but don't tell anyone about it"? Oh, believe me, it's not because you are special. Or actually, you are special, it's just that everyone else is too.

Speaking of everyone else being special, do you know who else is special too? You. I know, I know, it sounds like I'm trying to cheer you up with an obvious sales pitch, but guess what? It is also true. I'm sure you are special now because you were put on this earth to do great things, and one of those things was to pick up this book that will help you become a great nightlife entrepreneur. There might not be many people who read this book and actually start a career in the nightlife business. But you are one of the few who not only will pursue that career, but also you will be well known for it. People are going to look at you as someone they want to be like. You will become that guy or girl that sets the example. You will not only be known for throwing good parties and taking care of all your friends and clients, but people will also follow you for your ability to bring happy moments and fun memories to everyone. You are not the type of promoter who is in it for the girls or guys. You are the reason why I started writing this book. You are the one who might decide to write an updated copy of this first edition with new information so that up-and-coming nightlife entrepreneurs can continue to do this business for ages to come. You are one of the few who will understand that this is not just a job, and you are not just a nightclub promoter. You are the next nightlife entrepreneur. Therefore the responsibility to do us proud and rebuild our reputation is now in your hands. Maybe by the time you read this, we will have been successful at convincing local governments to require promoters to have a license. Maybe we will have brought a few classes to different colleges. Or maybe we'll have gone as far as writing a few more books on the subject. Whatever the case may be, I believe you will be part of this movement, and you will be remembered for it the way I wish to be remembered for it: not because my parties were great and people always had a good time, but because I left a legacy behind and was a local celebrity for years to come.

10

WHERE AM I NOW?

Can you believe we actually went as far as reading this whole book together already? Because I can't believe I actually wrote the whole thing. I have to start by saying that this has not been easy, but now that I'm on the last chapter of what I know will be a series of books that will go deeper into every important subject and also keep you updated, I just don't want to stop writing. I am very thankful that people like you took the time to read through it, and more than that I am very excited to see the things we might get to do together. The sky is the limit.

There is something I've been wanting to mention, but I didn't want it to get in the way of more important information. It is sort of a confession, but at the same time it might serve as a life lesson of some sort. It was almost three years ago that I decided to write this book, and I mentioned in the beginning the reason why I decided that I needed to write it then. I thought I would be able to do it in six months, but so many things have happened the past three years. If you recall, my main reason to get this done as quickly as I could was because my wife and I were blessed with the news of our first child being on the way. Today I can tell you a few things about that. The first is that Pierre Angelo is the biggest blessing that we could have ever expected in our lives. The second is that he is now two and a half years old and growing fast. We think we know how fast everyone grows until our child is born. The point I am trying to make is that I needed to get this done quickly because I did not believe that I would have the time when he arrived. Well, I was not wrong at all. The problem was that life got busy even before he arrived, so it was very hard for me find time to dig into these pages. The book was pretty far along, but I needed to finish it, and it just kept bothering me that I didn't have the time after Pierre arrived. Well, about a month ago I received news again: Pierre Angelo won't be alone at home anymore. Things are about to get hectic with the arrival of his brother and sister. Yes, twins. One plus two equals three, which equals a family of five. Therefore this book needed to get done *now*. So I decided to fix the procrastination problem. I even wrote a post on procrastination on my Word Press blog, *The Nightlife Entrepreneur,* *this is the link,* *https://thenightlifeentrepreneur.com/2015/06/05/tomorrow-is-not-always-there-stop-procrastinating/,* to help solve my own problem. I started to write the blog because I could write for twenty minutes a week, so at least I was doing something that did not look unfinished. But the book is so important and needed to get done for the future of our business, so I had to get off my behind and find the time.

I'm going to tell you a few of the things that have happened in my business in the past two and a half years. We decided that it was time for us to get back on the other side of the business, so we have been part of two new projects. The first is the Rubi Lounge in Brickell, Miami. We had the chance to be marketing and managing partners in opening this venue, and we were able to build a beautiful business. It was so good, in fact, that we received an offer to be part of another new project that included open-ing at least four new clubs and bars in different areas of the city. In order for us to do this, we had to let go of the Rubi project. We sold our stake in the business and opened the first Kukaramakara in downtown Miami. It's a Colombian restaurant, bar, and lounge with live music. I know it sounds weird, but it makes sense to our people! Now we are on to the second of the four projects and expect great things to come from these ventures. But as you may already expect, we had no time for so much responsibil-ity, so we decided it was best if we sold our stake in all these projects and dedicated our time to what we do best: marketing and promotions. Our current main mission is to find potential nightlife entrepreneurs who can build different nights in the different clubs with us.

This brings me to the next subject, which is the main point of this chapter. When I describe where am I now, I am talking about me, I am talking about you, and I am talking about anyone who decides to get into this beautiful business. You need to understand exactly where in you entrepreneurial life-span you are today. Me, I am in some ways on my way out. I just don't happen to be much of a promoter today, but as a nightlife entrepreneur, there is still more for me to do, like finding you and getting your career kick-started. I was one of the lucky ones to have started at the very beginning and lasted all the way to what I believe is the end of the promoter life-span. Notice I said promoter life-span, not nightlife entrepreneur life-span. The latter is a bit longer because there are other things you can do after being a promoter is no longer a valid option simply due to age and getting on with the next chapter in your life. But depending on where you find yourself in this life-span today and how well you follow advice, you might find yourself retiring very early. That is if you don't want to go on as a nightlife entrepreneur and do things like manage a club or own your own club, bar, or restaurant.

Let's start at the beginning of the life-span and see each of the stages the way I believe they should be divided, from my own experience. The years may be a little off, but it will give you an idea. Many careers have a life-span, and some are shorter than others. For example, typical baseball players have a career that ends around age thirty-eight if they are really good at what they do. Forty is pushing it unless you are a pitcher. But then we have a guy like Ichiro Suzuki, who, at age forty-three, broke Pete Rose's record for most all-time career hits. He looks thirty-five and says he feels twenty-eight. In the end age is just a number, but we will use age just to get an overall idea of where you should be. In the United States, the legal age to start working is fifteen years old, and although I started when I was seventeen, I had already done some successful events with high-school promoters. These events have become fewer over the years for different reasons, but they are very profitable if done right, and no law needs to be broken. These are events with no liquor sales but with a higher admission price. If you are between the ages of fifteen and eighteen, you should be doing these events. These are called "all-ages events" and cater to a younger demographic. The idea is to give high-school students the chance to experience going to a nightclub and get it out of their system without the need for alcohol. These events have a higher cover charge because you will not have lots of sales at the bar, so you need to make your money elsewhere. The demand is higher when the supply is very low. You will be selling nonalcoholic drinks, water, soda, and energy drinks. The music is usually provided by high-school DJs as well. Not long ago we put a team of high-school promoters together to start an all-ages series of events on Sunday nights when there was no school the following Monday. These promoters would bring a group of at least ten DJs for one event, and these DJs were even doing it for free. They just wanted the exposure, and of course they wanted the bragging rights in school. The crazy part is that some of these DJs went on to become great and very well known over the years. One now plays on the radio, and another is a local celebrity who plays for the Miami Heat. So it is also great to be part of the beginning of people's careers for that reason alone—believe me, seeing people make it and get famous is exciting. Even if nobody remembers they played at your parties, you will, and they shouldn't forget either. You never know when that might come in handy later on. Putting it all together is not that complicated. The secret ingredient is finding the cool kids in different schools and bringing them together in one event. Once they are a part of your event, you will have new kids lining up to promote for you. And this is where your mission to start building your team begins.

The second period in your life-span as a promoter is from ages eighteen to twenty. This is when you step up and start doing weekly events, but you do these at local bars and pubs. Remember that most of your clients will be in your same age group. It is very hard for a seventeen-year-old to promote to people in their late twenties, for example. So you will be doing events that cater to the same demographic as you are in yourself. The reason you work with bars, pubs, and even some restaurants when you're between eighteen and twenty years old is because while your clientele can't drink yet, they can already get into a lot of these venues. Nightclubs make most of their sales in pure liquor, but bars, pubs, and restaurants need to have food sales too. Most of them even have a liquor license that requires them to sell more food than liquor, and this makes your clients a good option for them. College nights are very popular among this age group. Most people start college around age eighteen, so you will have a lot of college freshmen and sophomores. These are the ones who believe they know it all, and the last thing on their mind is school. What is on their minds is Thursday night, college night. So build a good recurring Thursday party with a college crowd. This is where you start to build your regulars. College kids go out every night if possible, but it is best if you concentrate on one party on Thursday nights during those years. Go out on the weekend with different groups and build a following slowly but surely.

Happy birthday! You are now of legal drinking age. This is a big moment in your career. You can drink, sure, but the point is, so can your friends. The next period is your first one in the dog-eat-dog world. This is where you will start competing with other people, those who have been in the business and those who started with you. So remember to build good relationships with all of them. From twenty-one to twenty-five years old is the perfect age for a promoter to start his or her real nightclub promoter career. A lot of your clients will be young, and few will be big spenders unless something out of the ordinary happens. For example, in the past five years, there have been crazy politics going on in Venezuela. A lot of people have benefitted from this in a big way, meaning big money. This has created a new group of young Venezuelan kids who go out with Daddy's credit card and simply have no limits. I am talking about twenty-one-year-old kids with $10,000 tables night after night all over the place. This also affected the business in other ways because everyone wants to cater to those clients, so the deals that the promoters who work with that clientele get at clubs are just unheard of. It makes it very hard to compete. Well, thankfully for the people of Venezuela and for the business, things are starting to look up, and those people are not going as crazy as before. Also, law enforcement has started to look into it, since a lot of these kids are still underage. That is one thing that I will tell you: Don't go there. Do everything by the book and you'll have a longer life-span.

The next age is between twenty-six and twenty-nine. This is what I call a promoter's prime. By this time you should have a good client base, a lot of followers on social media, and a good reputation among other promoters, club owners, and more importantly with your clients and friends. Take advantage of this time. This is when you should be making the most money. If there is advice to be given about those years, it is save, save, and save some more. Don't go crazy spending the money that you will doubtlessly be earning. Don't go crazy living an extravagant life; there is no need for that. The most valuable things in life are still free, so use your money wisely. Go all out marketing-wise. This is when you need to have every event packed. There is no excuse not to. You should have some promoters with you, but you can do a lot of it on your own anyway. Don't rely on them alone. Make sure you do your thing, and they will learn to follow.

Between thirty and thirty-five years old, you will start to rely more on your subpromoters. This is when you need to start looking for the ones who will follow in your footsteps. See who has the right personality to be the next leader, not the next boss. Who is the one that would take care of your VIP clients when you are not around? Who is the one that will grow to be you one day? At this time, start to plan your retirement as a promoter. You will see that people beginning to follow you less. Don't feel bad; it is normal. They are simply growing too. Believe me when I say they want to go to every party, and they wish they were ten years younger the same way you will wish it too. But trust me when I say that it just gets better, as long as you have done everything in order, not skipped steps, and kept doing what was right all the time.

Then comes that age. In my case it was after turning thirty-five that I realized I was no longer as excited to attend parties, and I needed to go on to the next step. I would say that between the ages of thirty-five and forty is the perfect time to decide how you will leave a legacy behind. I decided to do it starting with this book, but I plan to continue by working with people like you. Today I am forty years old, and for the second time in my life, I feel like I am about to start on a great journey. I have been offered the opportunity to write the textbook for nightlife entrepreneurship and start a class at a local university. I am working with a close friend who is running for county mayor in the next election, and together we hope to re-quire people in this career to have a license, just like real estate agents take a test for the state. We will be regulating the business, but at the same time we will be making it a lot easier for those who take it seriously, and in the long run, it will be better for everyone. The best thing is to know that we will soon be able to be proud about what we do the way it once used to be. Having a nightlife entrepreneurship license will be something to be proud of, and it will also open many new doors. I know that by the time you get to this part of your career, things will already be better. That makes me feel good about what you and your team will be doing in the near future. More than that, I can't wait for you to leave your legacy and come up with your own new ideas that will make this even more interesting.

Now it's time to put down this book but not to throw it out. I hope that it served its purpose and got you excited about doing this with or even without me. The fact that you read the book is enough for me, but I am sure we can change the business together, and I hope to hear from you the moment you turn the last page. I mean that in the sincerest of ways. I also want you to think of who you would like to convince to do this with you. Remember how I mentioned that having a partner in this business is a good idea? Two heads together from a third mind that comes up with bet-ter ideas than either of you could ever have had on your own. I volunteer to be a part of your new lifestyle, helping you get started, opening doors for you, showing you how to find the right contacts, and so many different things. But I also encourage you to start building your team by passing this book on to the next person who deserves the opportunity to live one of the most wonderful lifestyles without working a day in his or her life and simply living in vacation mode all the time. See you on the other side. Cheers to your new life. Salud!

Made in United States
Orlando, FL
16 December 2022

26832911R00065